Fractured

WHEN YOUR RIVAL IS A CORPSE

Cinder Roherty

ISBN 13: 9781497336636
ISBN 10: 1497336635

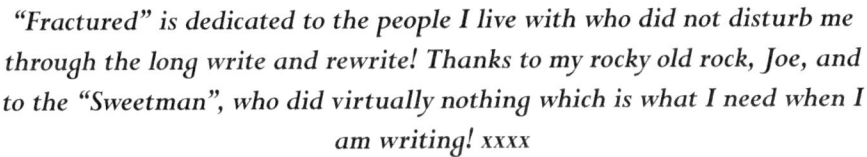

"Fractured" is dedicated to the people I live with who did not disturb me through the long write and rewrite! Thanks to my rocky old rock, Joe, and to the "Sweetman", who did virtually nothing which is what I need when I am writing! xxxx

Table of Contents

CHAPTER 1

The Almost-Kiss

Shelby lays back on her beach towel and stretches like a feline. The sun penetrates her young body, layer by delicious layer. Her friend's frolic in the water and on the raft, but Shelby wishes only to relax. It was a rare occasion when she does not have Andy to chase after—she almost feels guilty to be swimming without her little brother.

"*Seriously?*" Kiya asks, with disgust in her voice. "You're going to spend the afternoon curled up on a beach towel when you could be splashing it up with Jo-Jo?"

"Jo-Jo, Schmo-Schmo." She remarks lazily.

"I thought you liked him? This is not the way to show it, Shel!"

Shelby sits up and looks around. "Jeesh! Announce it to the world, why don't you?"

"At least then he would know you're interested." Kiya grumbles.

"I'm not sure I am."

Kiya sidles next to her bestie, letting sand slip through her fingers. "Since when? I thought you were smitten?"

"*Smitten?* What are we, like back in the dark ages?"

"Do you like Jo-Jo or not?" Ki asks, irritably.

"I don't know---he's got a terrible rep. He's always in trouble."

"But he's hot, right?"

Shelby looks at the boy in the water; showing off, as usual. Shades of the sun weave their way through his longish hair. Bronzed all the way down to the point where his swim trunks hang off slender hips and a desirable sixteen year old booty. It is obvious he is not bragging when he says he works out every morning and it has certainly paid off!

1

"Sizzling," she agrees.

"So--what's to think about? Why do you have to make everything such a big deal? You like him or you don't." Kiya says, sourly.

"He's truly not that likable."

"But the hot-ness factor more than compensates, am I right?"

"That, my friend, is a true statement!" Shelby agrees, standing up.

"Then get out there and lay it on him! He already told Matt that he would be willing to hook up with you."

"In that case, shouldn't he be laying it on me?"

In utter exasperation, Kiya jumps up and stomps to the water. Shelby decides she'd better join her before her best friend becomes her former best friend! Before she can get used to the water, funny guy, Jo-Jo splashes her! She will not give him the satisfaction of 'screaming like a girl' but she does turn her back on him.

"Nice view," he sniggers.

"That must be his idea of a compliment," she thinks, rolling her eyes. "He's a regular modern day Casanova."

When Shelby turns around, she is surprised to find Jo-Jo right there, within inches of her face. Arrogance aside, he is, at the moment, entirely compelling. She is alarmed when it appears he means to kiss her---right there on the beach, in front of her friends, God, and what appears to be her little brother barreling down the beach! Worst case scenario? Andy will be in the company of their father who has come to collect Shelby! Shelby does not want her first kiss to be in front of her dad and brother or Jo-Jo's dirtball friends! She imagines her first kiss another way; something special...and private.

"Shelby! Shelby! Guess what me and daddy did?"

"Hi kids," Representative Deacon Allison greets.

"Dad, you could have honked." Shelby is in something of a panic, with Jo-Jo looking on, smirking—not impressed by the Speaker of the Assembly himself!

"Shelby! Guess what daddy said? He said I could swim with you for a while!"

"I'm all done swimming today, buddy."

Andy's face droops. He looks down at the sandy beach and the gently lapping waves. His disappointment is palatable. She is willing to bet he has tears in his eyes but is such a tough-guy; he won't let anyone see them. Shelby can't bear to see her little love, her little brother, looking so sad! She relents, despite the look of mortification on Kiya's face.

"Ok, but just for a few minutes. Deal?"

"Shelby! Take me to the raft---puleeeeeze!"

"Andy, I'm already dry," she objects.

"I'll take him out," Jo-Jo offers.

"No, that's okay," Shelby quickly refuses.

"Shelby! Puleeze!"

Jo-Jo picks up her little brother and wades into deep water.

"Shelby, this water is cold!" Andy shouts, grinning.

"I'll bring the car around, honey," Deke tells his daughter, trusting her to keep Andy safe, as always.

"Ok, dad." Shelby does not take her eyes off the boys heading to the raft. She is not comfortable with Andy being in such deep water and starts wading out.

"Shelby! Shelby! Look at me!" Andy jumps around the raft like a carefree little monkey. Shelby grins at his antics until Jo-Jo jumps off the raft and makes for shore. Andy, standing on the raft alone, becomes hysterical! Shelby starts swimming, on her way to save the poor terrified little boy! After a stroke, maybe two, Jo-Jo goes back to the raft and reaches for Andy---it's all a big joke and he is chuckling at his feat, at his own meanness!

"Don't you touch him!" Shelby screams. "Don't you dare touch my brother!"

In minutes, Shelby is climbing aboard the raft. Andy clutches at his big sister. This time he is crying, with a vengeance.

"Is that funny to you?" she shouts. "Is it funny to scare a little boy?"

"It was just a joke, Shelby! Did you see his face when I bailed?"

"I did see his face," she agrees, calmly. Placing her foot on Jo-Jo's head, Shelby pushes him under. He comes up, spitting mad! Shelby positions Andy on her back and swims calmly back to shore. Jo-Jo stomps past them!

"That friend of yours is lame," he tells Kiya.

"She's too good for you!" Kiya defends.

Shelby, Kiya, and little Andy pack up and head to the car, where Deke waits patiently.

"Have fun, Andy?" he asks.

In response to Shelby's kick, Andy bobs his head up and down.

"Good, great. How about you girls?"

"It was fun. Thanks for the ride, Mr. Allison."

"Any time," the representative says pleasantly. Kiya hops out and Andy scoots over closer to his big sister. He places his head on her arm and Shelby rubs his short cropped blonde hair. When he looks up at her, she is forced to smile---Andy has to be the cutest kid on the planet! "Look at those freckles— he is a modern day Dennis-the-Menace!" He is Shelby's favorite person in the whole wide world!

"That damn Jo-Jo!" the girl who never swears, mutters to herself.

Like he does every night, Deke reads to Andy before bed. Sometimes Shelby sits in, but not tonight. She has to explain to her best friend why she wrecked her chances with Jo-Jo, *the dogfaced boy!* Kiya is an only child; she doesn't know what it's like to look out for another human being. She doesn't know what it's like to care for a motherless baby boy. Shelby does and she tries to do it just like her mom would have. She made a promise to her mom that last night; she swore she would always look out for Andy and it's a promise she means to keep!

"Good night, Shelby!" Andy shouts. "Shelby—good night!"

"Andy—you don't have to shout. Good night. Don't let the fire ants bite!"

"You shoulda answered me! Don't let the chupacabra bite!"

"Yikes! Thanks for that visual, Andy. Now I'll have nightmares."

"You can sleep with me if ya get scared," he offers.

"Thanks, buddy." Shelby leans in for her nightly hug and kiss.

Once Andy is safely tucked in, Shelby and her dad retire to the kitchen. "Popcorn?" Deke asks.

"No thanks; I'm going online for awhile. 'Night dad."

"'Night honey. I'll be home for dinner tomorrow night."

"You mean like every night?" she smiles. "Dad, can Kiya spend the night tomorrow night?"

"On a week night?"

"Dad, its summer vacay, remember?"

"So it is! What am I, like the absentminded professor?"

"Who?"

"Never mind honey, Kiya is more than welcome to spend the night."

"Thanks, dad."

Deacon does some of his best thinking on the drive to work each morning. Though Stoughton is a mere 19 miles from the capital, it takes an average of twenty-seven minutes to get to the hub of Wisconsin legislation. Thirty minutes of thinking; of solving the world's problems, not to mention his own personal problems, at seven a.m.! Another thirty minutes to unwind in the evening on his way home. He has his two favorite people in the world to go home to every night and that's exactly what he does. Even before Marissa died, leaving him the only parent of Shelby and Andy Allison, Deke was home every night. He insists upon having dinner with the kids every night and tucking them in. He avoids social functions whenever possible but if they're unavoidable, he will drive back to the city.

Deke makes his way past the protestors in the rotunda. This is a dedicated bunch; they have been sitting-in and singing for an entire year. He has to admire their dedication. Darcy, his secretary, is not at her desk when Deke arrives and he is surprised to find someone waiting in his office.

"Cress," he greets warmly. "What brings you by?"

"Nuthin' good," Cress Manchild answers. "Do you have time for a short interview?"

"Regarding?"

"What else—dismantling Obamacare."

"Uh, we don't have an appointment, right?"

"So that's how it is, huh?"

"Cress, seriously what more is there to say?"

"There must be quite a lot, Deke. This is the fortieth time they've tried to repeal it!"

"*Tried!* That's the operative word."

"Do they have a chance?"

"There's always a chance. They sure know how to waste tax payer's money."

"Can I quote you, Deke?"

"Slow press day? How is that quotable?"

Cress exhales wearily. "Damned if I know. They sent me up here, told me not to come back without a quote or fifty thousand dollars! Do you have either, Deke?"

"Unfortunately, I don't."

"That's okay. There are other jobs. I hear the UW Hospital is hiring maintenance people." She sighs dramatically. She's not usually into drama but desperate times call for desperate measures!

"In that case, the least I can do is buy you lunch before you're thrown into the medical field."

"Somehow that doesn't seem like quite enough, Deke. Could you throw in a Mercedes?"

"No Mercedes, but you might get dessert, just this once."

"Dessert instead of a Mercedes? That seems more than fair."

"White Horse Inn?"

"Great."

"One-ish?"

"Perfect-ish. Thanks Deke."

"No, thank you." He smiles sincerely at the reporter.

"For?"

"For always giving me a fair shake in the press."

Cress is always good company. She is intelligent, amusing, and a damn fine reporter. For some reason, he looks forward to this lunch all morning long. The White Horse Inn is just a few blocks off the square so State Assembly Speaker Deacon Allison decides to walk. A well known face in Madison, he is cordially greeted by many along his way.

Cress skids in about the same time Deke does.

"I was so tied up interviewing the protestors---one year later--- I thought I was late."

"You're right on time! As usual."

Deke and Cress order light. Both order draught beers with their club sandwiches and their conversation avoids subjects that might be considered controversial. It is off-the-record but they are careful not to place one another in an awkward position.

"How are the kids?" Cress asks.

Deke brightens when he speaks of his cherished children. Cress looks warmly on this man who clearly adores his offspring. A successful, worldly kind of guy, he refuses to leave the raising of his children to others, even though many 'on the hill' do!

"How come you never had kids, Cress?"

"I guess I never had time."

"I'm gonna call bullshit on that, Cress. If we waited until we had enough time or enough money, there would be no babies born. There are no perfect conditions to become a parent."

"I've honestly never found anyone I wished to procreate with, Deke."

"A beautiful woman like you?"

"Beautiful—right. Besides beauty does not necessarily make for a good mother."

"True but I think you'd be a superb mother."

"Based on what?" Cress asks, irritably.

"You're exceedingly nice. You're fun and you're smart---did I mention beautiful?"

"Possibly but it can never be said too many times." She smiles brightly at Deke and it warms him from the inside out. A simple little smile, he thinks, but why does it mean so much, coming from this spectacular woman?

"You're right. You should hear it every day. If you were my wife, I would tell you every day."

"Did you say it every day when Marissa was alive, Deke?"

"Definitely not as often as I should have but my regrets, with regard to my wife, are few."

"Not many can say that."

"I hope I have as much luck raising these kids—Shelby is getting to be at that age, you know."

"Trouble with darling Shelby?" Cress is astonished.

"Not yet but I understand it won't be long."

"I think Shelby will surprise you, Deke. She's levelheaded, smart, and devoted to you and Andy. Now Andy, on the other hand, may run you ragged---just because he's so energetic!"

"Tell me," Deke groans, leaning back in his chair and rubbing his belly. It's as flat as a teen's. Deke is a fine figure of a man Cress notices, and not for the first time. Tall, athletic, muscular---delish. Even though he notices her noticing him, Cress maintains eye contact. Something simmers between them until Deke abruptly looks away!

"Great lunch," she says. "Thanks."

"No, thank you---it was fun. It's always fun, Cress."

"You have no idea how fun it could get," she mumbles. If Deke notices, he does not respond.

"What'd ya get?" Dan Angus, The State Journal's editor, asks.

"Lots of good quotes," she remarks enthusiastically.

"I knew you were the right man for the job," he jokes.

"Lots of quotes and pictures from the *protestors*," she corrects his misconception.

"Cress, I was anxious to hear what your buddy, The Speaker of the Assembly, has to say."

"Hasn't that been a bit overdone?"

"Each time they try to overrule Obamacare, it's a new story. This is attempt number 40!"

"Everyone knows that already, Dan. We've beat that horse to death!"

"Not true. We have an election approaching and your buddy has never come out and taken a stand!"

"He's a democrat, for God's sake---isn't that 'stand' enough?"

"Uh—no."

"My buddy, as you call him, will not be my buddy long if I keep harassing him!"

"Deke's been around awhile, Cress---he knows the ropes, he knows the public has a right to know! Besides he's half in love with you."

"*What?!* No, he's not---the poor guy is still mourning his wife!"

"Oh please, *for four years*? Pull your head out, Cress—the guy is crazy for you."

"You're the crazy one, Dan. Deke is a one-woman man and Marissa was that woman!"

"I don't know what you're drinking but next time you're with him, check it out. And that next time, Cress? It better be soon!"

Cress develops a fiery gut in Dan's office. Usually a good judge of character, Dan is way off this time. As compelling as she finds Deke, she knows, romantically he is a lost cause. He hasn't been spotted with a single woman since Marissa died! He is entirely content to father his children and is completely devoted to the memory of his wife. It is just one of the many reasons Cress admires him.

On her way to the Capitol, Cress dials Deke's cell. "I'm comin' in," she warns.

"No—not right now. I'm in a meeting, Cress. Make it tomorrow morning, will ya?"

"Okay---think of something witty or funny about the dismantling---please!"

"I don't think such an animal exists---what could be funny about this travesty?"

"I don't know, Deke but my back is against the wall."

"I'll see what I can do."

Cress has what might be called a boy-toy. When she is super stressed, like today, he makes the tension go byby. The next call she makes is to Eric. She picks up beer and Hennessey and heads over to his condo. The darling boy answers the door in a towel. It takes Cress about 3 ½ seconds to dispense with that towel.

"You *are* pretty," she compliments, stroking him gently.

"No more than you," he says, unbuttoning her blouse. They kiss while Eric removes her clothing; slowly one item at a time. Each time they meet, he marvels at her small firm breasts and kisses each one. He runs a finger from her breasts, down her flat tummy, to the soft fur below.

"So soft," he purrs, cupping her tuft.

"Not to ruin the moment or anything, but aren't they all pretty soft, pretty much the same?"

Kissing the body part in question, Eric stops to give her question some thought. "Each one is as unique as the woman."

"Sweet talker," Cress grins, allowing him to go about his business. His business leads him to the moist cave. When he slides his fingers inside, Cress moans with pleasure. Pressing her against a wall, he investigates until he finds the sensitive hill which he plunders until Cress hikes up a leg. Eric boosts the other leg until she sits upon a divine welcoming party! His hand slides between their bodies and he manipulates her until she is arching against his hand. Recognizing her readiness, Eric drives her into the wall time after time, so fast and so hard, it actually makes her lightheaded! She closes her eyes, receiving him until she is entirely sated. Cress stays impaled upon the foyer wall for immeasurable moments until she can recover .

"My legs are like jelly," Eric confides.

"I'm probably too heavy," she says, trying to dismount.

"You're just so damn hot," he whispers, holding her leg so she can't run away. "I wish we could stay in this position all night."

"Me, too but unfortunately, I have a meeting tonight." Cress apologizes.

"You never stay the night," he complains. "Imagine the fun we could have if you would stay the whole night."

"I know but it would probably be suicide---you damn near killed me after only half an hour, Eric."

Eric helps her descend and she slides down the textured wall until she is standing. Her headache has disappeared and she feels loose, almost stress-free. "I owe you dinner," she promises, redressing.

"I'm not interested in dinner, Cress---unless you're the main course," he wheedles like the spoiled child he is.

Cress pulls Eric to her. She kisses him soundly on the lips before she turns to go. She feels a little guilty leaving so quickly but she has work to do! Eric, a trust fund kid, has nothing better to do than hone his skills with different, willing women every day. His reputation in the boudoir---or up against a wall—is well known, Cress reminds herself.

Cress spends three hours back at the office investigating voting records for dismantling Obamacare. She hopes to find someone else, someone as reliable and as well respected as Deke, to interview. The lines were drawn just about where you might expect---Repubs voting no, Dems voting yes for Affordable Healthcare. There are a few representatives who claim to be neutral, she notices. Deke, The Speaker of the State Assembly, wishes to remain fair to both sides of the aisle.

That's what makes him so newsworthy---that and the fact that he can be quite outspoken when he gets riled up! Cress wishes she had a shot at riling him up.

One voting record is so erratic; Cress thinks this representative bears looking into. Paul Neuman, no relation to the actor, from the 44th district, is so unpredictable, you never know which way he might vote! "Interesting," Cress thinks. She is willing to bet she can get an interesting quote regarding Affordable Healthcare from this guy. That will get her off the heavily burdened back of one Deke Allison! Unfortunately, it's after midnight---she will have to wait till morning to tackle Mr. Neuman.

For a millisecond, she contemplates going back to Eric's but she knows she has already been replaced and three in a bed is just too much crowd for Cress! That fantasy is not on her bucket list but she has plenty of others...

Once sequestered in her lonely bed, Cress thinks of Eric. Her hands slide over and stop on her breasts which seem to push against her palms. She rubs taut nipples and revels in the pleasure she feels. Her hands glide down her stomach, bypassing her navel until she is at the juncture where left leg meets right leg. Her fingers find the sensitive spot but she is reluctant to pleasure herself although she has done it before to relieve stress. Spreading lotion on the area, her well practiced fingers slide across the 'happy place'. Briefly, Cress remembers the things Eric did to her but her thoughts soon wander to another area, almost rocking her world!

Cress's thoughts center on doing these very things...but with Deke Allison! She knows he would be gentle, considerate and thorough. She imagines him naked; erect with desire for her and her only. She wishes she could reach out and touch him as her hips began to move under their own power. She imagines her fingers are Deke's lips and that visual does her in! Whoosh!

"So good, so good," she moans, drifting off to sleep.

CHAPTER 2

Cress's Crush

*I*n the morning, Cress upbraids herself for her uncouth behavior. Even though he is a young forty, Deke Allison is not looking for another woman! There will be no other woman for Deke and she may as well get that through her thick skull! She has to stop fantasizing about him; it could spill into their work relationship.

Armed with that positive thought, Cress heads over to Deke's office, where she prays he will throw her on his desk and ravage her! So much for ending those fantasies...

"Good morning, Cress!" Deke bellows, with good humor.

"Good morning---why so cheerful?"

"Seeing you always brightens my day."

"No, seriously---why so upbeat this morning? What's happened?"

"As Craig Ferguson says, "It's a great day for America!"

"You watch Craig Ferguson?!"

"Minimally," he admits.

"Good thing or I'd kick you off my bucket list."

Deke moves closer to Cress. He is so close she can feel sweet coffee breath on her eyes, on her eyelashes. "I'm on your bucket list?" he asks, seductively.

So nervous, Cress cannot think of a quick come back or a joke of any kind; no snarky response! She merely stands still and absorbs the essence that is Deke. She feels his body heat. She wishes...

"Today America wins---the vote left Obamacare intact!" he enthuses, taking a step back.

"Speaker Allison, may I quote you?" That dang story getting in the way of Cress's passions!

"You bet your bippy you can!"

"That, I will not quote---no one says bippy anymore, Deke."

"They don't? *Are you sure?*"

"Whatever you do, don't say it in front of Shelby or her friends---they'll crucify you!"

"Point taken, Cress. Thanks for the heads-up!"

Cress and Deke sit for many minutes until she gets the entire story. The gist of it being that even though they are crippled by a Republican Governor and Senate, the people of America will get the affordable health care they deserve! This is Deke's cause; Cress can feel his unbridled passion.

"Wish those passions were directed elsewhere," she silently complains.

"I knew you'd get that story, Cress! You didn't have to do anything unsavory to get it, did you?"

"You're a regular comedian, Dan. Unlike you, Deke Allison respects women!"

"Ouch—hey, I respect women! As long as they put out."

Having submitted her complete story, Cress exits the building. Walking round the square to cool down, Cress thinks of swinging by Eric's again. That always relaxes her but her mind continually flits back to Deke—she wishes *he* were willing to relax her! She looks longingly at the capitol; she knows he's in there.

The long ride home is unusually uncomfortable for Deke---he keeps thinking about Cress Manchild. He thinks about how small and fragile she seemed when he stood close to her. He remembers she smelled like patchouli oil--- how he'd loved patchouli oil in college! All the college girls wore it, including Marissa. He flipped on the radio so he could concentrate on world affairs instead of a woman he *could not, would not, dare not have!*

He almost comes undone when he remembers she said he was on her bucket list! On her bucket list---did that mean she wanted to 'do' him? Deke feels his pants getting tighter by the mile. It isn't something he's experienced in nearly four years! It's an encouraging-discouraging feeling.

Shelby is teaching Andy to jump rope in the driveway when Deke pulls in. Seeing his kids cools his lust…in a huge hurry. It is slow going with Andy jumping long before the rope gets to his feet. Shelby is quickly running out of patience but Andy will not give up! "I can do it!" he shouts, over and over.

"Maybe we could try again tomorrow," Deke suggests. "Maybe get ready for dinner?"

"I'm not eating dinner until I can jump rope," Andy informs them.

"I, for one, am hungry," Shelby grumbles.

"I'm hungry, too!" Deke agrees.

"I'm not hungry! I want to jump rope with my friends tomorrow."

"We could get up extra early," Shelby offers.

"I'm okay out here, dad. I just want to do this!"

"That's why we have a microwave, I guess," Deke tells his children. He is proud of Andy for working so hard to achieve a goal. "You come in when you get hungry, son."

"Want a drink or anything?" Shelby asks, reluctant to leave her little brother alone in the driveway.

"I'm ok."

"What a maniac!" Shelby tells her dad over dinner.

"He's one of a kind, that's for sure. When he decides he wants something, he'll work for it. You're both like that."

"Dad, how am I like that little mutt outside? I mean, really?"

"What about the violin. Shel? You would not put it down the first two weeks you had it! You still practice daily and have now mastered it! That is the same determination your brother is showing out there."

"I hate to be the one to tell you, dad, but I am a long way from mastering the violin. I just muddle along---but I do love it."

"Look how determined you both were to ride a bike. Neither would stop till you learned to ride alone."

"Dad, where does that stubbornness come from—you or mom?"

"A little of both, I guess. I'm more intense than your mom was; she was more laid back but you dared not cross her!"

"Did she have a temper, dad?"

"Rarely but when she let loose, look out!"

"What kind of stuff made her fighting mad, dad? I can't remember. I was almost thirteen; I should be able to remember her!"

"Don't try so hard, it will come back to you. Anything thing that could be harmful to you or Andy or our family turned your mother into Mike Tyson! No one was going to harm her cubs."

"She called us that, didn't she? I remember that now." She smiles thinking of her mother.

Andy drags himself in from outside. He flings his rope on the table and gulps down his milk. He is sweaty and his face is dirty like he might have been wiping away tears—Deke and Shelby won't ask about the tears.

"How's it going, slugger?" Deke asks.

"I almost got it, dad! That damn rope is too slow!"

The minute, the nanosecond, the word "damn" slides out of his mouth, he freezes! He cussed in front of his dad! His dad is gonna use that rope to spank him! Andy is surely a dead man—not that he's actually ever gotten a spanking but he never cussed in front of his dad before, either.

"Andy!" Shelby mouths, too shocked to speak.

"Daddy, I'm sorry! I didn't mean to say the bad word!"

"Try not to use it again, ok?" Deke cautions, not getting fired up about a minor slip of the tongue.

Andy releases the breath he has been holding. He looks wobbly enough to cry which is something Deke hoped to avoid.

"Want me to go back out with you?" Shelby asks, rescuing her little brother.

Andy nods, walking back to the driveway.

"Poor little bugger," Deke thinks, feeling for a small boy trying to act like a man. He's only six; he has a ways to go!

With no success achieving his goal, Andy comes in for his bath. At bedtime, Deke brings him a peanut butter sandwich to munch on while they read their nightly story. While Andy chews, Deke reads. Usually they take turns reading but they find peanut butter is not conducive to reading aloud.

"I'll read tonight. You read tomorrow night. Deal?"

Shelby has had quite enough family time for one day and stays in her room the rest of the night. She is not only ducking her family, she is ducking Jo-Jo and Kiya. Her best friend is still trying to hook her up! Apparently Jo-Jo does the dumping; does not like being the dumped-upon. To quote her baby brother, Shelby doesn't give a damn what Jo-Jo wants!

She is slightly comforted hearing the drone of her dad's voice, reading to Andy. They're lucky their one remaining parent spends so much time with them, loves them so intensely, Shelby thinks, gratefully. She wonders momentarily if her dad ever gets lonely; if he ever misses having a woman in his life.

Unbidden, Cress's face appears before Deke on his way in to work. "Pretty little girl," he thinks. "That wild mane of auburn hair, a mask of freckles across her nose, lips that are full but not Botox full---just kissable full. That's it, Deke---no more lunches with that one!" he warns himself.

When Marissa died, Deke swore off love and the opposite sex! He'd had his fire, his passion and it had been enough to last a lifetime! Marissa was the lid to his pot, the ying to his yang and how she'd laugh, hearing him put it so awkwardly! Deke is devoted to his children and to public service. His is a full, satisfying life---how dare this gorgeous reporter make him feel so restless!

That night, when Eric calls asking Cress to come over and exercise, she does a weird thing. She tells him, "I'm holding out for a hero" and disconnects. For some reason, she thinks she means it! She goes directly to Deke's office to invite him to lunch—lunch is no big deal, right? They've done at least twenty lunches---what is one more lunch among friends?

"Why, Cress? I have no more quotes for you today although your story made me sound smarter than I actually am! Thank you."

"Does there have to be a reason? I owe you lunch---end of story!"

"Can't do it today---I've got committee meetings all week."

"What about breakfast?" she asks, quietly.

"I don't usually eat breakfast---do you?"

Cress stands directly in front of Deke's desk so there will be no room for misunderstandings. "Deke, I was thinking maybe dinner at my place and then, I could make you breakfast in the morning."

Grasping the meaning of her words, Deke stands stock still. Cress Manchild, the cutest, smartest reporter in all of Madison Wisconsin, is actually propositioning him! He is definitely titillated and finds he would so love to take her up on the offer! Until, he thinks about his kids and then he thinks about Marissa and then, God help him, he thinks of how long it's been; worrying he may just be out of practice! The whole appealing, exciting, thrilling idea of it is just too risky--on so many levels!

"I am so honored," he begins.

"Deke, I'm seriously not up to this "but" so spare yourself and let me save face—I get it!"

"Cress, every single night, I tuck my children in, after I've eaten dinner with them. Afterwards, I read a book with Andy. I kiss them good night. This is a ritual I am unwilling to break, as much as I'd like to take you up on your very thrilling offer."

"That explanation makes this slightly more tolerable," She mumbles.

"You are so desirable. Another time, another place I would do back flips to be with you but I take my responsibilities seriously."

Walking blindly out of the capitol, Cress sits on a nearby bench on the square. She's shaking, she's so embarrassed! She is honestly mortified! She'd laid it all out there, risked her heart and her body, only to be shot down by a refusal! Oddly, she doesn't hate Deke for rejecting her but how will she ever face him again?

Eric picks up on the first ring. "Did you drink all that Hennessey?" she asks. "No? I'll be right over!"

On the way to Eric's, she relives her embarrassment and tries somehow to improve on it. Her comeback could have been so clever, she thinks with disgust. It was useless; no matter how she rearranges it, she still comes out looking like a schmuck! Hopefully an afternoon workout with Eric will take her mind off of Deke and her humiliation at his hands. Eric lets her in but she can see he is little cranky---she doesn't have time for cranky. What's more, she doesn't care if this diva is cranky or not! She came to forget her troubles!

"Hennessey?" she asks.

"Last time you didn't stay long enough for one drink," he pouts.

"Don't talk, Eric---just start licking! You start at one end and I'll start at the other."

This idea so appeals to Eric, he forgets why he's peeved. He leads her to his king sized bed. He lays back and watches her unceremoniously strip down.

"You could at least work it a little," he complains.

"No pole," she snaps, climbing into bed.

"I've got your pole, Cress," he promises.

"That's why I'm here, Bucky," she mumbles, kissing him.

From his mouth, Cress kisses her way down his neck to his hairy pecs. Hard, tiny nipples quiver under her attention. Skimming over the hairy regions, Cress comes to the good part. Eric seems mighty happy to see her but she can't get into her exercise regimen the way she usually does.

A good sport, she covers him with her mouth. Eric wriggles on the bed, wildly excited because Cress has never put her mouth on him before! He doesn't last long and Cress crudely spills his seed out on his belly. Eric pulls her to him and begins his assault on her body—hands cupping her breasts. He slides his hand between her legs to find she isn't even damp!

At first, he feels like he's let her down but eventually, he sort of gets into it. Cress doesn't want to fool around at all but she goes along anyhow. It turns out to be kind of hot. She lets him do what he wishes and he does not miss seeing or kissing any region of her body. When Eric is ready, he pulls Cress on top. She sits upright and accepts Eric's intrusive member. It is a bit dry but Eric finds he is excited enough for both! He rocks and lurches until he is spent. Feeling as though she is doing some sort of penance, Cress lets Eric have his way with her all night long. It is mostly just plain embarrassing and she gets not one iota of pleasure from all of his probing. When Eric awakens, Cress is gone. He has a feeling she won't be back.

"Two wrongs do not make a right," Cress reminds herself for three days in a row. She is morbidly ashamed she so freely gave herself to Eric: not for love, not for fun, but just for some skewed sense of penance. It won't make her more appealing to Deke; probably just the opposite. She is not normally a self destructive girl but she hoped her time with Eric would help her forget the m, m futile crush.

For weeks, Cress works hard to cover the Capitol. Between the year old demonstrations and the new arrests of singers in the Rotunda, there is plenty to report. One of the singers for peace suffers a heart attack when he is arrested. That is newsworthy—particularly newsworthy since he is a pastor! She is careful not to run into Deke but still manages to do her job to Dan Angus's satisfaction.

Deciding to go the extra mile, Cress makes it her business to check on the pastor. She goes to the hospital and the soft spoken pastor explains nonviolence is the only way to go! He is about to be released so their conversation is brief and far from inspiring. She thanks him for his time and tries to think of a more interesting angle for an article. Dan will have an assignment for her but she wants to carve out her own legacy at the paper.

Stopping by the hospital cafeteria for lunch, Cress almost goes into cardiac arrest when she sees Deke in line ahead of her. She takes several steps back, hoping like hell that he hasn't seen her.

"Cress!" he calls before she can escape.

She pastes a grin on her face but her cheeks burn in embarrassment. She pitched her idea; it was shot down---simple as that! Still, it's hard to face Deke---especially when he looks so scrumptious, so strong and handsome and hardy!

Coming towards her, Deke smiles and holds out his hand. "There you are! Join me, will you?"

She does not mean to lie to this sweet, sweet man but she is fiercely protecting herself from a broken heart! "I would love to but…"

"Don't tell me you don't have a minute for an old friend? I've missed you, Cress."

Cress smiles, picks up a diet soda and slice of pizza, and joins Deke. Naturally he is eating a salad. Just another reason it would never work out, she tells herself.

"Where have you been? I've heard Cress-noises around the capitol but I never run into you anymore!"

That's the idea, she thinks. "Cress-noises?" she smiles.

"Of course I've read your stories but apparently my opinions no longer interest you?"

Everything about you interests me, she thinks. "I decided to stop hounding you."

"You make hounding tolerable, Cress. Pleasant, if I am to be truthful."

"What's the deal, Deke?" she asks irritably. "I laid it all out and you refused me. Now you're sending me mixed signals---or am I misunderstanding *again*?"

Deke leans in and quietly tells her," You are not misunderstanding me, Cress. I was a damn fool that day but I do have certain obligations to my children. I promised Marissa I would be there for them and by God, I intend to do that! I can't do slumber parties. I have to be home at night."

"Every night, Deke?"

"Every single night---I promised, besides I think it's important. It helps them feel secure—at least, I hope it does."

His second refusal makes Cress admire him even more. "You're a wonderful father, Deke."

"I need you to know, I am honored by your invitation. I haven't dated since Marissa died but if I ever were to, you would be the one I would choose—I mean it, Cress."

"If that is the case," she mentions shyly, "it seems like there might be some sort of resolution so everybody gets what they want."

"I can't think what that might be…"

"Deke, it hasn't been so long that you've forgotten about 'afternoon delight,' have you?"

Deke looks a little embarrassed but also intrigued. "I don't want to take advantage, Cress. You should be wined and dined and paraded round the city!"

"I wasn't asking for all that, Deke."

"But that's what you deserve—you deserve respect. Besides, I am not a casual affair kind of guy."

Cressida wonders how much respect he would have for her if he found out about Eric, about last night—the meaningless and crude sex. She hopes he will never, ever learn her true character. She scoots closer to Deke.

"Have you ever tried one?"

"A casual affair?"

Cress nods seductively. "Sometimes casual affairs turn into something more lasting," she whispers. Her breath on his ear makes him quiver. Deke put sexual desire in a drawer four years ago. Today that drawer seems like Pandora's Box as it threatens to burst into the fore! He has a consuming urge to kiss Cress.

"How's your afternoon?" she asks.

"Pardon?"

"This afternoon---are you free, Deke? I live nearby…"

Deke pushes his salad and his fork away. Without a word or a nod of assent, he stands and follows Cress from the hospital. She is too excited to talk so they walk three blocks, in silence. At the bottom of the stairs of her West Wilson Street apartment, Deke hesitates.

"Are you sure this is what you want to do, Cress? You're a young, beautiful girl---why me of all people?"

Cress reaches for his hand and gently pulls him up the stairs. At her door, she actually fumbles with her keys like a untried virgin! Deke takes them from her and with a steady hand unlocks the door. This beautiful man is not going to slam her up against a wall, she thinks. Sex with Deke will have all the trimmings and she can scarcely wait!

As if reading her mind, Deke reaches for her. He holds her close and tips his head so he might kiss her. The kiss is tentative, his first in four years, but he quickly warms to the activity. His tongue invades her round, willing mouth, flickering back and forth, reaching for hers. Cress arches towards him and he uses his hands to press her closer. Huge hands splay across her bottom and her back. He expels a loud groan and almost seems embarrassed by his renewed passion.

Cress leads him to the bed where they sit; very prim and proper, for approximately three seconds. Deke lies back and pulls Cress with him. She finds herself sprawling across him when all she wants is to get naked so she might get as close to Deke as God intended woman to do. She's wanted this beautiful man for as long as she can remember!

Deke slides his hands under her shirt and her skin burns where he touches her. She climbs higher so she can press her body into his. She can feel his passion already but no one is more ready than she! Deke starts to unbutton her blouse and Cress helps him; so very eager! He gasps when she slips out of her blouse and then her bra.

"You are as beautiful as I imagined, Cress!"

"You imagined me shirtless?" she asks, sitting astride of him.

"I've imagined you naked many, many times but you are more beautiful in person than in my fantasies."

"Truly?"

"I thought you could tell—I always stared so much."

"I don't recall any staring or any indication that you were picturing me naked, Deke."

"Thank God you didn't look under the desk."

Cress laughs at the visual he's created. She leans down and presses her breasts to him; he covers them with his hands and Cress rubs against him.

"These obstacles must go!" he insists.

"You mean our clothing?"

Awkwardly, Deke tries to undress while Cress sits upon him. To expedite things, she climbs off and drops her pants.

"Cress, let me." Deke slides her panties down. Every few inches, he places a kiss on the spot where they had been. Once the flimsy panties are removed, he goes to work on his own clothes.

"Ahhh, silky panties," he says, tossing them in the air! He kisses the furry little muff before pulling her onto his lap. Cress wraps her legs around his waist and slides down on Deke's very hard and impressive member.

"You fit like you were made for me," he gasps.

"I was made for you, Deke!" she states, emphatically.

"I don't want to disappoint you, Cress. It's been so long since I was with a woman…"

"You could not disappoint me. I am so into you. I'm ready for you, Deke."

Deke raises and lowers Cress on his shaft, sliding her slowly over his erection. It isn't long before he erupts! Cress almost beats him to the punch: she's wanted Deke for so long, she can hardly hold on! She clutches onto him after the sex, until it is decided that they should lie down.

"I could have done that better; Cress and I will prove it! Just give me a few minutes."

"Deke, if you do it any better, I'll be in intensive care," she jokes.

"No honey, I'll make it more memorable. I promise."

"It cannot be more memorable. This is the day, the moment I've waited for."

"Really, Cress?"

"Honestly and truly. I've been after you a long time, Mr. Speaker."

"Why me—you could have the greatest guy in the city."

"I just did! Are you fishing for compliments?" She teases.

"Hardly. But seriously, why me?"

"You *are* fishing! I wanted you because you are: handsome, worldly, funny, and smart! Now I can add 'good in bed'".

"I would take any one of those things but today, I'll go with 'good in bed!'" To prove it, Deke rolls on his side and runs his hands up and down her side. His touch is feather light and Cress rolls on her back so he might have better access. He runs one finger down her body from her cheek, to her neck, to her sternum, over her right breast, and around her nipple until she moans. Taking a more direct route, he ventures over to her left breast, giving that nipple equal treatment. Slowly his finger wanders downward, circling her navel, until he reaches the downy softness of her feminine core. Cress never takes her eyes off Deke;

still amazed to be lying in bed next to him! Several fingers get in on the action, wending through the lushness that is Cress.

She holds her breath as he goes further, coming upon the mound and then, moisture as he slides his fingers inside. Cress arches her back in response and lets out a breath. As Deke's fingers move inside her, her hips take on a life of their own—undulating, circling, reaching for satisfaction. Deke does not let up and despite good intentions, Cress cannot hold out for him to join her!

"Why didn't you join me?" she whimpers. "I wanted us to finish together."

"Cress, I have no appointments this afternoon, do you?"

"No." she admits, excitedly biting her lip.

"I haven't enjoyed a woman's company in a long time—I believe I'll need the whole afternoon to catch up."

"It would be an honor to do my civic duty," she teases.

Doing her part to update the Speaker of the Assembly, she reaches for the once-again engorged phallus. He groans when she takes it in her hand. He damn near has a heart attack when she covers his member with her mouth! She works it with her tongue, swirling, suckling, licking. Soon she gets down to business as she tries to take it all in her mouth; deeper and deeper. Unfortunately, she cannot absorb it all! Withdrawing momentarily, she goes back down! She moves so Deke doesn't have to and it isn't long before the pressure builds to the point that he cannot wait a minute longer. He bursts like a frozen pipe in Cress's mouth. She swallows it down, without a second's hesitation.

"I see you've done this before," he says, as a joke.

Cress wonders exactly how guilty she actually looks. Will she be expected to tell Deke just how many times she's actually performed oral sex? Her look of mortification is misconstrued; Deke is afraid he's slandered her!

"It was just a joke, Cress! I just meant because you are so good at it. I didn't mean…"

"It's ok," she lies and for the first time in her life, she is ashamed of her promiscuity! "No, that was the first time. I just got lucky." she jokes.

"You're sure a quick learner."

Cress hopes he will leave it at that and move on!

"Got anything to drink?" he asks. "I'd forgotten how thirsty a good workout makes you."

"Of course," she said, hopping out of bed.

"I wish you'd do that again," he says, lying back on the pillows.

"What?" she asks, fearfully.

"Hop out of bed like that---it sure is cute."

"Water, beer, orange juice, or diet coke?"

"I better go with the coke. No beer for me until the kids are in bed."

"I don't think it's bad for kids to see their parents indulge in the occasional beer."

"Me either. I just don't do it. That's me."

"Your kids, your choice."

"True, that."

"You sound just like a kid," she notices.

"Comes from hanging out with teenagers!"

"Teenagers? As in more than one?"

"Well, Shelby's buddy, Kiya, all but lives with us. She's there every day."

"Is that annoying?"

"Not at all. If Shelby is in a good mood, the entire household is in a good mood."

"She's not one of those permanently PMSing girls, is she?"

"Thankfully, no, but she likes to have her friends around."

"That sounds reasonable."

"I thought so too."

"What about the singers getting arrested?" She is excited to hear his take on the non violent protest.

"That was some BS, wasn't it?"

"What is the big deal about peaceful demonstrations in the rotunda?"

"Power trip. It could have been prevented, though, if they had gotten the permit."

"That makes it alright to handcuff and arrest senior citizens?"

"Of course not; that's where the power trip comes in. I can hardly wait till the elections! We'll get this state straightened out!"

"That makes two of us, Deke." Cress hands him a diet coke and a huge glass of ice. She wants to talk politics with him but there are far more pressing thing to discuss----*like the placement of his penis!* She climbs over him to get in bed. He stops her midway. She is so slight, he can easily rub her against himself—back and forth, back and forth until once again, they are both in a lather and her breath comes in small spurts. She opens her legs, eager to receive him. Deke does not hesitate and they made slow, leisurely love. The rushing is over—at least for today.

Cress places her head on his shoulder. She knows their time is coming to an end---Deke has children to feed and homework that needs doing. She also has an article to work out but all she wants to do is make love to Deke. Usually everything takes a backseat to her work but… that was before Deke!

"I wish I could stay…." he begins.

"I understand Deke—just go." She says quietly.

"Can I come back?"

"Forty thousand more times," she grins. "But that's it!"

"That's it? What if I come knocking on the forty thousand and first day?"

"I will have to revise the rule; maybe make it a guideline!"

Deke leans in for a kiss before he departs. Cress fights an unreasonable urge to pull him back in bed.

"I'll call you, if that's ok?"

"Please do. Shall I walk you to the door?"

"If you do, I'll never leave."

"In that case, I better stay undercover."

Before Deke hits the landing, Cress already misses him. She touches her face; red and sore from whisker burns. She touches her lips; swollen from passionate kisses. She touches her breasts; tender from hours and hours of foreplay. She touches the core of her femininity; sensitive from the sensual battering it took all afternoon. She thinks about Deke being right there, impaling her while she begs for more!

Her fingers toy with the area. She presses on the spot Deke kissed and suckled and she begins to heat up. Her hips rise and fall as she manipulates her own body. She is thinking of Deke, wanting Deke, but the pulsating need is of her own creation.

CHAPTER 3

Gruesome Grandma Florida

Deke tries not to think of Cress on the long drive home. Every time he does, his pants get tight and uncomfortable. He cannot enter the house springing a chubby! Especially with his mother-in-law in attendance; her car blocking his garage, as usual.

"Crap! What does she want now?"

Grandma Florida, as the kids call her, never got over her daughter's death. Her only consolation is that she sees Shelby and Andy almost every day! It irks her that Deke is alive and well and her poor, darling Marissa is gone. Deke understands her sorrow completely but it doesn't make her any less objectionable.

"Daddy!" Andy shouts, jumping into Deke's arms.

"Hi buddy! Shel! Florida!"

"Dad, can Kiya stay for dinner? Netta says there's plenty."

"I don't see why not. Kiya rarely misses a meal."

"Dad!"

"I didn't say it like it was a bad thing."

"Good! Oh, Grandma's staying for dinner too."

Blindsided!

"If that's ok, Deke?"

"Me casa…"

"Daddy, you smell different!" Andy comments.

"No, I don't."

"Yeah you do, dad. You smell like patchouli oil," Shelby confirms.

"Where would I get patchouli oil?" he scoffs.

"That would have been my next question," Florida remarks, scrutinizing her former son-in-law.

"It must be that new air freshener I bought for the car."

"I love patchouli oil," Shelby remarks.

For one brief moment, Deke remembers how much he loved patchouli oil this afternoon! He catches Florida staring at him and knows he must not get carried away with his reminiscing.

Over dinner, Florida lectures Kiya and Shelby about not getting involved with boys, not ruining their reputations, and when all else fails, getting on birth control!

"Uh, Florida, I think these girls are too young to be thinking about birth control."

Kiya and Shelby bob their heads in embarrassed agreement.

"By sixteen, some girls already have two kids! Obviously *their* grandma did not give them fair warning!"

"Who are these kids with kids?" Kiya asks. They all roll their eyes. Kiya hasn't learned not to ask questions. All Florida wants is everyone in the whole world to agree with her!

Florida looks over the top of her reading glasses at Kiya. "What does your grandma say about birth control Kiya?"

"My grandma would drop dead if she even heard the words birth control and Kiya in the same sentence! Besides she lives in Florida."

"Well, burying her head in the sand won't solve anything!"

"Florida, what is there to solve?" Deke calmly asks, before Grandma Florida shines a light in Kiya's eyes or gets out a rubber hose!

"Maybe you don't care if Shelby gets knocked up but I do!"

"Shelby doesn't even have a boyfriend and she is not going to get knocked up! When she gets a boyfriend, we will do whatever is necessary."

"Oh, I'm sure. You come in late, smelling like perfume! I'm sure you'll know when the time is right!"

"As usual, I was on time tonight so we could all sit down and enjoy a family dinner. I haven't missed one since Marissa went away. Patchouli oil is not perfume but if I came home smelling like a sewer, it's my business! My kids, my business!" He says for the second time today.

"These kids are my business too. My blood runs through their veins!"

"Florida, you are a guest here. Do not forget that." Deke's voice has a hard edge to it.

"Grandma, daddy comes home to dinner every night," Andy volunteers. "Then he reads me a story---then, he tickles me! And grandma? *My blood is my blood!*"

The kids all ask to be excused at the same time; Kiya and Shelby try hard not to laugh at Andy's remark.

"Your brother is so weird," Kiya tells Shelby.

"No, he's not! That comment proves he's highly intelligent."

"Weirdly intelligent then!"

"Kiya you are a guest here. Do not forget that." Shelby says, repeating her dad's words. The girls snigger. "*But seriously*, don't call my brother weird."

Before Grandma Florida leaves, she steps into Shelby's room. "Well, I'm leaving now, Shelby."

"Ok, byby grandma," Shelby says cheerfully.

"Shelby," she says quietly, "you call me at once if anything untoward happens around here!"

"Untoward in what way, grandma?"

"Your father is acting peculiar…"

"I don't think dad is any different today than he was when mom was here," Shelby defends.

"You're a loyal girl, Shelby but there is definitely something afoot---have women been calling here for your father?"

"Uhmmm, sometimes his secretary, Darcy, calls. Why? What does that mean?"

"It all boils down to the secretary, doesn't it?"

"Grandma, what do you mean? Darcy is a middle aged grandmother. Dad doesn't have a girlfriend, he really doesn't."

Florida runs her hand over Shelby's hair. "Poor naïve little girl. Well, I'm off but I'll be back! Your father will not keep me from you!"

"Dad would never keep us from you."

"Well, it won't work if he does!"

"So by by, grandma. I better go check on Andy."

"Another disappointment," she sighs.

Shelby retraces her steps. "What's that supposed to mean?"

"He obviously didn't have time to be influenced by your mother and now look at him; he's a disrespectable little renegade."

"That is not true! Andy is smart and sweet, just like mom!"

"Oh dear, what a hostile home this has become! I am on my way out."

Shelby turns her back on her grandmother and does not turn around until she hears the engine of grandma's car fire up. "You old biddy," she whispers.

"So, Shel---let's just say your brother is not a weird little kid but what about that grandma of yours? What a pain in the ass."

"Can't argue with that one, Ki."

The girls spend the rest of the evening texting boys. Jo-Jo's name pops up periodically but Shelby does not read his texts.

"How long are you gonna string him along, Shel?"

"Is that what you think I'm doing, Kiya? I'm just not interested; plain and simple."

"Seriously? You hardly know him!"

"I know him well enough to know he's a jerk. I don't have time for jerks, Ki."

"Not even hot jerks that look like they could model underwear?"

"A jerk is a jerk; and they stay a jerk their whole life long!"

"I'd like a go at that jerk," Kiya says with real longing in her voice.

"Feel free… but prepare yourself for heart break."

After Andy's story, Deke lays down awhile with his little boy. The small sleeping boy looks so much like his mom, it makes Deke's chest hurt. It was Marissa's greatest regret; that she would not live long enough to raise her children. She knew Andy would forget her and it broke her heart while her body dissolved before their very eyes.

"I'll talk about you all the time, honey," Deke promised.

"For awhile, you might."

"Your memory, your bravery will always be a subject of conversation in this house. Shelby will strive to be the woman her mother was. Andy will ask for mommy-stories and we will supply them! If he doesn't ask, we'll relive your life for him. And, my love, not a day nor night will go by that I do not miss and love you!"

"Until you find someone new, someone you will love more than a recollection." She sighed.

"You, my dear, are the only woman for me. You know this." Deke leans in and kisses his failing wife.

"That's not what I want for you, Deke. I want you to have love and passion in your life. Just every once in awhile, think of me and maybe smile."

"I have had love and I have had great passion, Marissa---enough for a lifetime. I will do my best to raise our children with the same care you would. It is enough, more than enough!"

"You deserve more, Deke but please always put the kids first."

"I promise."

As her pain mounted and her horizon seemed more blurry, Marissa reached for Deke's hand. "It has been a damn good life! I'm glad you were part of it, Deke."

"I wouldn't have missed it for the world." He choked out the words.

Marissa has a few final moments with her daughter before she falls into a restive coma. Even in a coma, pain plagues her as cancer chews at her gut and gnaws at her bone marrow. Her passing comes as a relief to Deke; at last, his beloved is at peace! Now to make Shelby and little Andy understand…

CHAPTER 4

Rumors on the Hill

This morning, Deke feels like he has a new lease on life. Nothing like a dose of afternoon delight to put a smile on a guy's face, he thinks on the drive to the capital. He remembers stunning red tangles and carpet that matches the drapes. He luxuriates in the memory of taut, compact breasts and rocklike nipples; more than a mouthful, to be sure! His cock stiffens when he remembers the feel of Cress sheathing it. The ride to work is suddenly uncomfortable as he moves and adjusts to accommodate memories of the unforgettable rendezvous. He worries he should be feeling guilty but knows he has Marissa's blessing. He is happier than he has been in years—all because of an incredible woman by the name of Cress Manchild!

There is a spring in his step as he passes through the rotunda, dodging protestors and the press. He knows the moment he speaks to any of the singing protestors, his photo will be splashed across Madison newspapers and he will be considered a traitor by the Governor!

"To Hell with him!" he thinks, shaking hands as he passes through to his office. Darcy is waiting with hot coffee, a bagel and just a touch of cream cheese; just the way Deke likes it.

"Thanks, Darcy. How far am I behind today?"

"Well, Deke you just got here." The question has her puzzled.

"That never stopped my constituents before! Or the haters either."

"There is truth in that statement," she agrees, with a smile.

Deke seems different to his secretary; looser, more relaxed. Whatever's happened, she hopes it will continue; she likes her see her boss feeling good.

As soon as Darcy exits his office, after one scalding gulp of coffee, Deke places a call to Cress. "Good morning, gorgeous!"

"You sure know how to start out a girl's day!"

"I aim to please! Did I?"

"Did you what?"

"Did I please you?"

"Oh, you old compliment fisher—you know you did! I dreamt of it, in fact."

"I dreamt of it while I was still awake—even during Andy's storytime! Don't ever tell him, ok?"

"As if I'm likely to tell a six year old his dad had naughty thoughts while he read 'The Little Engine That Could'!"

"This little engine wishes he *could*...right now."

"This little caboose would be willing to stoke his engine!"

"Stoke his engine?"

"Damned if I know, Deke. I was trying to make an analogy. I didn't come close to pulling it off, did I?"

"Good effort, though. When can I see you, Cress? I can't wait to see you, to touch you, to kiss those delectable lips!"

"If I say this afternoon, will you think I'm easy?"

"I will think you're magnificent but today is not good for me. Meetings all afternoon."

"Then home for that family dinner."

"Yes, indeed. How does your schedule look for Friday?"

"As you know, I mostly make my own schedule so I will say yes to Friday and promise to stay wet till we meet again!"

"Wetness...a damn fine quality. Till Friday."

Cress throws him a private little kiss; a kiss no one will ever see or receive. She sits back in utter contentment until Dan Angus steps into her cubicle.

"What's that look, Ms. Manchild?"

"What do you want?"

"Is that any way to talk to your boss?"

"You're only here because you want something. It must be big because it's a whole thirty step walk from your office."

"As always, you are very astute, Cress."

"Cut the crap, Dan—spill it."

Dan would have made himself comfortable but every surface was piled high with books and notepads and even a couple of laptops. "So, okay," he says, pushing over a pile of Cress's clutter so he can perch on the corner of her desk. "I once suggested Deacon Allison, your pal, has the hots for you. It appears I was in the right pew but the wrong church. From what I hear, there *is* somebody out there he's interested in---I want you to expose them!"

"All of a sudden, we're a tabloid?" Cress acts brave but inside, she is quaking.

"The public deserves to know!"

"Why? The guy is unattached; he can see whomever he chooses!"

"What if the woman in question *is attached*—the constituents deserve to know."

"C'mon!" Cress scoffs. "Who, honestly, cares?"

"What if it's political? What if she or someone else is setting him up? What if they get Mr. Speaker in a compromising position and blackmail him? What if they insist he votes their way? Lots of potential for scandal here, Cress."

"Are you reading John Grisham again? Patterson?"

"Funny—not! Look, I know you like the guy but look into this for me, will ya? We won't use it unless it's absolutely unavoidable."

"Give me a flipping break, Dan! If you came across the story on your mother's love life, you'd run it! At least don't insult my intelligence."

"Just check it out!" His stay is short and far from sweet.

"Check this out," she whispers, extending her middle finger. "Dan!" she calls out. "What makes you think he's seeing someone?"

"A good Samaritan called in a tip."

"Good Samaritan, my ass!" she thinks. "Seems like someone is trying to discredit the Speaker but that's not happening on my watch!" To make sure, she places a call to Deke to forewarn him.

"Maybe you shouldn't come by on Friday---it appears they're watching you."

"Nothing will keep me from seeing you on Friday, Cress but I will be discreet. Don't worry; this too shall pass. Listen honey, I have someone in the outer office. I'll see you soon."

"Of course. I only called to warn you."

"Appreciate it."

"He sounds just like a politician," she thinks. "I'm from Wisconsin; I know a snow job when I hear one!"

Friday is a million hours away for two people who long for one another. Thursday night Cress goes to bed early just to finish off the last day before Deke comes to make her day! She isn't sure if that light tapping is her heart hammering in her chest or if someone is at the door. She chances it and answers the door.

Like Dick Tracy, Deke slides through the front door, past paparazzi, past random voters, past potential voyeurs until he's inside, reaching for Cress. His large hands envelope her waist and he pulls her to him, probing moist lips. "Missed you so much," he mumbles.

Standing on tip toes, Cress's answer is a carnal invasion of his mouth, his throat, and his sensitive ears. They cling to one another after two days of no physical communication --just like randy teens. Deke backs her up until she feels her bed against the back of her legs. Gracefully, she falls back, pulling Deke with her.

"How long?" she asks through frantic, needy kisses. "How long do I have you?"

"I'll have to leave in about three hours to be home on time," he says, pulling her shirt over her head, marveling that such a perfect specimen would want to mate with him!

"I can do a lot with three hours," she says, wetting her lips.

"*We* will do a lot with three hours, my love." He corrects.

"I like how you think, Deacon," she whispers, unbuttoning his shirt, laying it neatly on a nearby chair.

"I like everything about you," he confesses.

These words are like symphonies to Cress's ears; this extraordinary man finds much to like in her! She's halfway in love already but she will never tell Deke, terrified of scaring him off. She talked him into his first fling—she didn't say anything about love, just lovemaking. Quickly, they shed their clothes and take delight in one another's bodies.

"You're so lovely, so perfect, you could sell undergarments in a catalog."

"I'll remember that if this reporter gig doesn't pan out," she jokes.

"But you're good at that, too, Cress---you do everything perfectly."

"Let me show you…" Cress brings out a small bottle of motion-lotion and drips just a tad on Deke's upright member. Her hand slides up and down the pole until he is gyrating on her bed, calling her name. Very lightly, she places a well aimed kiss on the tip.

"Honey, that will be bitter for you," Deke objects, panting hard.

"Kiwi flavored," she grins. "Bought it especially for the occasion."

"Ahhh," he groans as she licks the small helmet and finally places the erect penis in her mouth. She absorbs the kiwi as her mouth slides up and then, right back down! Over and over, she services him, one hand cupping underneath.

"Cress," he mutters. "Come up here, please. I don't want to do it without you."

Happy to be included, Cress seductively climbs the length of him until his cock is sequestered neatly between her legs. The ramrod stiffness nestles against her femininity and she slithers up and down his pole until she is mad with desire. They cry out with what can only be ecstasy from a well ridden ride! Cress crumples on Deke's chest. He runs his fingers over her hair and tries to catch his breath.

"You're remarkable," he enthuses.

"You inspire me."

"No, you inspire me to be more creative; I was never very creative in that department. I feel kind of bad about that now."

"Knowing you, Deke, you were probably always a considerate lover and I'm sure Marissa was more than satisfied."

"You're very kind, Cress. I didn't mean to bring her to bed with us—I was not thinking of her when we made love."

"I know. She's here but not in a disturbing way. I don't begrudge what you had with her, Deke."

By way of a response, Deke's hands travelled over Cress's backside, pressing her into an already erect member. She moves around a bit; creating some friction, and finally climbs on, tightly enclosing his remarkable penis. Deke groans, feeling the snug fit surrounding his hardness. As Cress rises and falls upon him, Deke works his hand between them. He massages the small sensitive nub, resulting in a new frenzy of passion. Sensing that she is close to the end, Deke drives deeply into her, sending her straight over-the-edge, into carnal oblivion. His hands stay fixed to her bosom even after she rolls on her side.

"May I take these home with me?" he asks.

"Of course, we'll bag them up before you leave!"

"You are quite accommodating, Miss Manchild."

"Don't let that get out, okay?"

"That I would never do; I would not want to share these delectable breasts, these delicious lips with anyone."

"Nothing to worry about, Deke. It took me so long to get you in my bed, you're lucky I allow you to leave."

"Speaking of leaving," he says guiltily. "I will have to soon---the kids are expecting me."

"I know the drill, Deke---don't feel guilty. Your kids need you at home at night. I totally understand."

"So sweet," he says, kissing her brow. "I cannot take you out on the town but no one says I can't take you to lunch, Cress."

"It's not necessary, Deke."

"Nonsense. You and I have been doing lunch for a long time—it's business." He says, kissing her and sitting up to find his shoes. "Tomorrow? The Governor's Club? About noon?"

"Governors Club? Uh, no. That's just asking for trouble but I would love a sandwich from The White Horse Inn---a place I've come to think of as 'our place'."

"The White Horse Inn it is---noon?"

"I can't wait!"

"The only drawback is that I won't be able to touch you." Deke says, sadly.

"I'll be right here when you can." She whispers.

Deke gathers her in his arms. "I hate to leave you."

"No more than I but I have to kick you out---you're gonna be late!"

"Thanks, love."

Cress feels such profound loneliness when Deke leaves, she can't believe it! How has the Speaker wormed his way into her heart so quickly, she wonders. Maybe he was there all the time...

CHAPTER 5

Let's Try This Again

*L*unch at the White Horse is fun and casual, as always. Cress is entirely relaxed, joking with Deke like they do every time they lunch. They eat light but as usual, they both have a beer with their sandwich.

"Today, honey, I have to go back to work," he says sadly.

"I figured," she admits. "Maybe tomorrow," she says her eyes lighting up at the idea.

Deke's smile warms her.

"Well, isn't this cozy!" A harridan screeches, drawing all eyes to their table. "This must be the source of all that patchouli oil!"

Cress has no idea who this loco woman is and how she knows about the patchouli oil she wears. Deke just looks pissed.

"Excuse me, Elise but I'm in the middle of a business lunch and you are out of line!"

"Looks more like monkey business to me! Is this the woman who will replace my poor deceased daughter?"

"Don't be absurd! Cress is conducting an interview for The State Journal, an interview which you have effectively ruined!"

"You may be able to fool some of them, Deacon but I see how you look at one another and my daughter is not yet cold in her grave!"

"Are you going to sit down or are you going to continue to make a scene?"

"I won't sit with your whore."

Deke stands up and faces his mother-in-law, "You owe this reporter an apology. You owe me an apology. Marissa wouldn't have condoned this kind of behavior!"

At the mere mention of her daughter, Elise becomes pale and her lips get wobbly. Cress feels so sad for her; she cannot stay another second!

"Deke, I'll call your office to reschedule our appointment," she says, rushing out.

"Cress…" he watches his lady love depart as his mother-in-law dissolves into a puddle. This must be that tangled web they speak of…

"Deke…" Elise begins.

"I know, Elise," he says, placing a kind hand on her shoulder.

Appointments done for the day, Deke finds a moment to contact Cress before he heads for home.

"Hi baby," he says softly.

"Deke."

"On a scale of one to ten, how mad are you?"

"Zero. I'm not mad at all."

"That was very uncomfortable; I'm sorry."

"It was probably more uncomfortable for that grief ridden woman."

"That is true but Cress, it's been four damn years!"

"Could you get over losing Shelby in four years time, Deke?"

"Jesus! Of course not! I would never get over it!"

"That's where Elise is now."

"God Cress, you don't pull any punches, do you?"

"I thought you knew that about me," she remarks quietly.

"I do but you brought it right to my front door! Talk like that scares me; I'm so afraid it will jinx my family!"

"It did."

This conversation is really a downer and Deke is almost sorry he's called to apologize for Elise's behavior.

"Listen, I've got to get going, I don't…"

"Want to be late---I know the drill. Go home, hug those kids."

"We'll talk tomorrow."

The ride home is worrisome for Deke. He doesn't want to rock the boat with Cress but he has an uneasy feeling that she may be ready to bail. He realizes he has a lot of baggage; much for any woman to contend with. "It's not all hard dicks and wet champagne," he reminds himself.

"Daddy!" Andy drives his head into Deke's gut before he leaps into his arms.

"Hey, buddy---missed you. Where's Shel?"

"Talking to her boyfriend."

"Shelby has a boyfriend?" Deke is once again blindsided.

"Jo-Jo," Andy says, giving his dad the skinny on his sister's love life.

"Jo-Jo? That's a name? It sounds more like a circus monkey," Deke mutters.

"Haha," Andy chuckles. "Circus monkey! That's funny, dad!"

"What's so funny, squirt?" Shelby asks. "Hi dad."

"Nothing's funny," Deke says, trying to cover his butt, giving Andy 'the eye' which is completely ignored.

"Daddy said…" he falls down, still laughing.

"Andy, is that Ryan out there? Go check."

"No one's out there, dad," Shelby insists.

"Daddy said Jo-Jo sounded like a circus monkey!"

"Gosh dad, that's mean—you don't even know him," Shelby says. She hates exhibiting righteous indignation over someone she doesn't even like, can't actually pull it off, so she leaves the room!

"Shel," Deke calls, speaking to her departing back. "It was a joke!"

"It was funny, dad!" Andy approves.

"Andy, your dad does not have good people skills today." Deke is disgusted with himself on so many levels.

"What's that supposed to mean?"

"I wish I knew. C'mon, let's try to lure Shelby out for dinner."

"Ok, dad---what's lure?"

"What are you, about six years old?" Deke jokes.

"I am six! I really am!" he jumps around like the aforementioned circus monkey.

Shelby comes to dinner as though she has been gravely affronted. "Honey," Deke says, passing her the salad. "It was just a joke. I didn't even know you had a boyfriend. Hey! How come I didn't know you had a boyfriend?"

Shelby makes a face at Andy who is quite adept at ignoring any sort of criticism. "I believe I'm old enough to have a boyfriend, dad---all my friends already date!"

"The best defense," Deke thinks, "is an offense. That's how girls operate; Marissa had been no exception."

"No argument there but I thought you might have told me, Shel."

"Dad," she admits, seeing his sadness. "I don't have a real boyfriend---Jo-Jo and I are just talking. When I get one, you will be the first person I tell---you and 'the mouth' over there."

"That would be great, honey---thank you but don't feel in any hurry. Boys are just like busses; another one always comes along!"

"I think you've mentioned that before, dad," she grins at her overprotective dad.

Dinner is a quiet affair. Shelby helps clear the table before heading to her room to finish her homework. When Grandma Florida calls later that evening, Andy yells for Shelby. Deke and Andy continue watching Duck Dynasty until it's time for Andy's bath.

"Dad," Shelby says, through the closed bathroom door. "When Andy goes to bed, I need to talk to you!"

"What's up, honey?" Deke's says, going to the door.

"Not now, dad—after Andy is asleep!"

"Shelby, is everything okay?"

"Dad, please can we talk later? In private?"

"Depend upon it, Shel."

Dekes thoughts return to Shelby and the urgency of her request—is she still mad about the circus monkey remark, he wonders? Andy seems unusually wild tonight and unwilling to go to sleep. He keeps Deke with him longer than usual.

Deke quietly knocks on Shelby's door. "Honey—do you still want to talk?"

"Is Andy asleep, dad?"

"He is—finally."

"I don't want him to hear this." She seems down and Deke has to wonder why.

Sitting on the side of her bed, Deke waits for Shelby to begin. She is looking down and it is awhile before Deke realizes she is crying. "Honey, what is it?"

"Dad, is it true? Is it true you have a girlfriend?"

"So--your grandmother *has* been up to no-good again!"

"Is it true, dad? Grandma said she saw you together!"

"Shelby, your grandmother interrupted an interview I was having with a reporter from the State Journal. Cress and I have had multiple interviews at that very spot for many years and that is what your grandmother saw! Naturally, she jumped to the wrong conclusion."

"She said your eyes were bright and you were excited!"

"Oh Shel, your grandma has not been the same since your mom went away."

"Neither have I, dad! Mom has only been gone for a few years! Didn't you love her, dad? Didn't you love her enough to forget about other women?"

"I did. I do and just as you promised, I will let you know if I ever decide to date again. Right now, it's not a consideration."

"Really dad? Because grandma said..."

"Your grandma lost her only child. She makes me mad, always looking for trouble, but I can't blame her."

"I lost my only mother—I will never accept another mother, dad. Not even for you."

"I would never ask you to, honey." Deke gets up and goes to Shelby at her desk. He leans down and hugs his little girl; she clings to him and sobs. He is so mad at Elise for using this child to further her own selfish agenda!

"Was grandma lying then, dad?" she sniffles.

"Your grandma was mistaken. I explained it was an interview; she chose not to believe me and then, she concocted this lie."

"Dad, do you still miss mom?" She asks, looking into the eyes of her only parent.

"Every day---how about you?"

"Same as you, dad, every day but then, sometimes, I can't remember her. I can't remember if her eyes were blue or grey or if she smelled like cinnamon or lemon. Does that make me a terrible person, dad?"

"Of course not---it makes you human. When I feel forgetful and guilty for being forgetful, I remember her kindness and love for us all. She would forgive us for forgetting if she had blue eyes or brown; we're not meant to be perfect, Shel."

"Sometimes when Andy asks me about her, if I don't know the answer, I make up a lie—his whole memory of mom is a lie!"

"I doubt that, honey, but it gives him something concrete to hold onto---does it happen often? Does he ask for her?"

"No, not often. She has been gone more than half his life—he's pretty much used to it."

"It's a damn shame when a six year old doesn't even have a chance to know his mommy!" Deke states. His kids got short changed and it still makes him mad as hell!

Deke can see he is losing Shelby by the way she keeps turning her attention to her computer screen. Although he knows he is lying through his teeth, Deke feels better for assuaging Shelby's fears. This thing with Cress could just be a fling; no point in rocking their tentative boat, unless absolutely necessary! Deke says good night to their only daughter, wishing Marissa was there to help them all survive her demise!

Later in bed, Deke alternates between sadness for his children and memories of Cress, sitting on him, rocking his world! It feels unseemly to think of both at the same time but there it is---his dick has *a mind of its own!* How wild and untamed she looked perched upon his swollen manhood, just like Lady Godiva herself! Magnificent! He thinks of her day and night; thinking only of his kids more often! What does it mean—he's been out of circulation for quite awhile? Is this the start of love or merely an infatuation?

"Whatever it is, it's pretty strong," he thinks, with a smile and about half a 'woody'.

In the city, Cress thrashes and tears at her bed clothes. Comforter on the floor, comforter on the bed—pillow flying through the air! Thanks to Elise Van Horn, she is having a helluva night; one riddled with guilt and lust and even a little fear!

"What if Deke feels she's just not worth the effort or the potential for scandal? What if I never see him again, never know his kiss, his warm embrace?" She feels like weeping for a loss that has not yet occurred.

"Big dummy!" she scolds, not sure if she means Deke or herself.

Finally she falls into a fitful rest and dreams about a beach and a certain tall, good looking public servant. He is nude and all his magnificence stands at attention, the sunlight bouncing off his rigidity. All eyes are trained on her fantastic lover but he holds interest only for Cress, offering her the security of his embrace. They turn and walk towards the sparkling sea. When they are thigh high in the surf, Deke turns to her, pulling her close. Their lips meet, part, and meet again! They dissolve into the water until they are slightly adrift, their passion keeping them afloat!

"Their passion keeping them afloat? Did I write that, she wonders. It does not sound like the vernacular of reporter Cress Manchild! Am I turning into a cheesy romance novelist, then? Is that what love does to the otherwise sane?"

"Wait---what?! Who said anything about *love*? This started out because I wanted a single night with Deke Allison. I accomplished that and boy, was it worth waiting for! Time to move on, Cress---this guy is out of your league."

"Not yet," she whispers in the dark. "Let me keep him a little longer, please."

All day long the lovers fight the urge to call... Deke is rattled by Shelby's proclamation that she will never accept another woman in their lives. He does not want to upset his kids; they have been through more than their fair share. He cannot choose his happiness over theirs, even if it means being alone. Still, he wishes he could talk to Cress, maybe explain, maybe there will be no reason to explain---maybe she gets it. She understands what the kids mean to him and poses no pressure. God, he misses her!

Cress remembers when Marissa was still alive; seeing her and the kids around the capitol. She had a smile for everyone even though Andy hung on her like a baby Kong. Shelby was a beautiful child; the kind you see in commercials. Marissa is gone but those babies are not and they need their daddy like never before. Resolutely, Cress determines to back away and let this family continue on its journey towards mental health---if only she can.

It is forty-eight hours since Elise ruined their lunch. Deke is miserable and takes solace only in dinner with the kids and story time with Andy. Even if he cannot reach out and touch Cress, he wants to hear her voice. Right or wrong, he will call her once the kids are settled down for the night.

All resolve flies out the skylight when Cress hears Deke's voice. "I probably shouldn't be calling but I had to."

"I hoped you would and then, I hoped you wouldn't," comes the flat reply.

"So, we're on the same page?"

"Unfortunately but Deke, don't worry about me---just worry about Shelby and Andy."

"What if I could do both?"

"I think we both know that won't fly."

"I don't know, Miss Cress Manchild, I learned a bit about aeronautics in college."

"So you are a pilot-wannabe?"

"Something like that; mostly I just want to set my own life course."

"It's a worthy ambition but tough to achieve when little people are involved."

"For someone who claims not to be mother-material, you are quite astute when it comes to the feelings of children. I like that."

"I like children, Deke, I just don't want to destroy another human being with my ineptitude."

"I disagree and I think we should discuss it over lunch---tomorrow."

"Oh God no, not another lunch!"

"Cress, I cannot let Elise or any other small minded person dictate where I will eat my lunch or with whom."

"Deke, after that scene with that unfortunate woman, I can't go back to The White Horse Inn."

"There are other restaurants in this great city, Cress. Please don't let her run you off!"

"OK, Nitty Gritty, my treat. Or is that too open, too many people, too many constituents?"

"I haven't had a Gritty burger in years; sounds fun! See you at one o'clock—does that work?"

"At least we know we won't run into your mother-in-law there," she smiles into the phone.

"If we do, we'll know for sure that she's stalking us."

"Do you think she is, Deke?"

"I don't know; grief is a powerful thing. But don't let it ruin our date, honey."

"I'm game. See you at one."

"I could come and collect you," he offers.

"And lose your primo parking spot? No way—besides if my boss got wind of a luncheon date, it would be front page news tomorrow!"

"The State Journal is now a tabloid? Who are we—Wisconsin's version of the Kardashians?"

"I asked the same question! I think Dan will do just about anything to keep the paper alive---newspapers are just about obsolete, you know."

"Isn't that a bitch? A fine newspaper like that? Cress, I hate to ask but where do reporters go when newspapers go under?"

"We become paparazzi and annoy simple folks like us, folks just trying to have a sandwich!" She jokes.

"That's what I love about you, Cress—your unique perspective! I'll see you tomorrow---check the bushes for Elise." Deke warns.

Signing off, Cress wonders if she heard Deke correctly---did he say the love- word? Not I-love-you, of course but hearing the love-word coming out of Deke's mouth is a wondrous thing! She returns to work with a big goofy grin on her face!

CHAPTER 6

No Nitty in Her Gritty!

"Who was that on the phone—your boyfriend?" Dan asks.

"What is this—middle school? What's your deal lately, Dan?"

"What's yours, Cress? You've lost your edge."

"My edge? In what way have I lost it?"

"You used to be like a pit bull, you would do anything, go anywhere to get your story!"

"I still will."

"To a point."

"Meaning?"

"There are now certain elements of the news that are off-limits." Her boss speculates.

"Whatta got for me, Dan?" Cress wants to avoid delving any deeper into this conversation and specifically, her personal life.

"Nothing very exciting, no interview with the Speaker or anything—you don't need an appointment for that anyhow, do you Cress?"

"I am free to drop in on the Speaker and any other member of congress---what's your deal, Dan?"

Dan Angus stands to his full height. "I might ask you the same, Cress. I told you once the speaker was half in love with you---was I right?"

"Mind your own business! Give me my assignments and don't worry about my private life, Dan!"

"So, that's how it is, huh?"

"That's how it is! We're not friends, we're not confidantes, you're just my boss---end of story."

"I can live with that, Cress—if I can trust you to get me the story."

"I am a professional and you have no right to doubt my integrity!" Cress stomps out of Dan's office with a huge chip on her shoulder---how dare he!

By one o'clock, she has calmed down and waits for Deke in a booth at the Nitty Gritty—it smells so good in the restaurant and the joint is jumping, like always.

"Hi beautiful," Deke says, folding his height into the booth. "Sure wish I could kiss you."

Seeing him, Cress bursts with pleasure. "No more than I."

"Did you beat the bushes before you ascended the stairs?" He jokes.

"If I am to be perfectly honest, I did scrutinize those scraggly bushes out front when I passed by."

"Me, too!" Deke chuckles. His laugh is infectious and Cress finds herself beaming. "Are you hungry?"

"I-can't-wait-to-sink-my-teeth-into…" Cress murmurs.

"Girl, you're killing me!" he tells her. "And I have a full day ahead of me—can't get out of it!"

"That's okay—Dan is sending me on some wild goose chase, just to show me who's in charge."

"What's that all about?"

"He thinks I'm withholding something, wants me to spill my guts about you and me."

"You and me? How does he know there *is* a you and me?"

"Damned if I know—maybe Elise called him."

"Are you serious? Because anything is possible with Elise."

"No, not about Elise but he is suspicious for some reason, thinks I'm withholding a story."

"Weird, we really are Wisconsin's Kardashians!"

"All over a simple little sandwich and some chit chat!"

"Its nuts but imagine if they knew how badly I am craving you right now?"

Looking at her lover, Cress feels moisture pooling between her thighs. His eyes scan her body and land on her sumptuous breasts; nipples spring out of nowhere stretching against her shirt.

"How much time did you schedule for lunch today, Deke?" she whispers.

"I usually take an hour."

"That gives us forty minutes to get to my apartment and get naked."

Deke tosses a few dollars on the table and rises to leave. "Crap, I walked---that will cut into our time."

Handing him her keys, Cress says, "My car is parked in the ramp. Just get in like you own it. I'll hold back a minute---are you game?"

"I was born game! Don't dally---I'm gonna need a good twenty minutes to make you forget all about that Gritty burger."

When Cress reaches her jeep, she suggests Deke slump down a bit.

"I'm not slumping, Cress. I am a grown man, able to make decisions for our state and for my own affairs! Please proceed."

In a matter of minutes, they are securely stationed behind closed doors.

"Ummmm," Cress groans. "Sure could go for a Gritty Burger."

"How about a Wisconsin Bratwurst instead?" Deke jokes, rubbing his stiff member against her tuft. Cress opens her legs a bit and it reaches the sweet spot, immediately sending her into orbit. Her moisture makes it slide with ease, over and over, until she is weak with want.

"You better lie me down," she orders.

"But what if I didn't? What if we stayed just like this? I can hold up a little bitty thing like you."

To prove it, Deke hikes her up by her buttocks until she is neatly, deliciously impaled upon his erection. She tightens, loosens, tightens, loosens until Deke arches and slams up into her. They rock it until they are happy to forget all about lunch. Cress, something of an authority on standing-up sex, slides down but stays attached. With Deke still embedded within her, they do the crab walk until they arrive at her bed.

He lays her on the edge of the bed and bends to attend to her. From his position off the bed, he moves slowly and steadily inside her. So caught up in the action of the moment, Deke does not miss a beat when Cress brings her legs up until they are resting on his shoulders. It changes things up a bit and he plunges deeply inside of her repeatedly until they are both exhausted---but happy and deeply relaxed.

"Best lunch ever!" he says, resting for a minute.

"Good time allotment, Mr. Speaker," she says, looking at her alarm clock.

"I like to think I can 'git her dun'!" he jokes.

"If it ever comes up for debate, I will be happy to give you a testimonial."

"I need you on the campaign trail," he whispers, kissing her ear. "I'm sorry…"

"Deke, I know the drill, please don't apologize. Just think of me when you are at one of your meetings and smile, pretend like you actually give a crap about what they're pushing."

"Depend upon it, my love," he says, pulling on his tie and jacket. With a kiss, Deke heads up the hill where he will try to give Wisconsin his best shot!

Pressured by Kiya, Shelby agrees to go to the Mall with Jo-Jo. She meets him at the Food Court where she finds him slamming down pretzels and root beer.

"Hey," she says, standing uncomfortably by while he eats.

"Hey," he says, concentrating on dipping his pretzel in the nacho cheese.

Shelby feels awkward and ready to flee. Promising Kiya she will give it one more chance, she plunks down, without a proper invitation. The ill-bred idiot does not make a token offer of food; just gobbles it up with no regard to his 'date'.

"Nice," she says under her breath.

"Whatdya wanna do?" he asks, wiping his hands on his jeans.

"What are my options?"

"Whadya mean?"

"Do you want to eat---no, you already did that! Do you want to shop? Do you want to see a movie?"

"I got no money---how about you?"

"You came to the Mall with no money?"

"I always do." Deke never allows Shelby and Kiya to go to the Mall unless they plan to shop. He feels hanging around the Mall with no money leads to shoplifting and trouble. As usual, Shelby is surprised to learn how in tune to teens Deke actually is.

"I guess we could walk around, talk."

"About what?"

"I don't know, what do you and Avery talk about?"

"You!"

"*Me?*"

"Well, girls—we talk about girls. What we want to do with girls."

"Huh. Did you watch the State of the Union Address last night?" Shelby asks, moving on.

"No, why would I?"

"You live in America; he's our commander-in-chief."

"You're a weird chick; good thing you're so hot! You'll never keep a boyfriend talking like that!"

"What should I talk about, Jo-Jo?"

"How about me," he says, leaning in and puckering up.

Stepping back, Shelby gives him the "eyw-look". Jo-Jo receives it loud and clear.

"This is not how I pictured our first date, Shelby," he confesses.

"Is it how you imagined out *last* date, Jo-Jo?" she asks, pivoting and heading out.

Startled, the boy stands at the Food Court wondering exactly what just happened. "Your loss!" he shouts.

Shelby wishes she had the courage to flip him off; instead she keeps on walking.

Kiya is disappointed in Shelby when she hears about the disastrous date. "Every girl at school, from freshmen to seniors, would jump at the chance to kiss Jo-Jo!"

"They are welcome to him!" She doesn't say so but she does not wish her first kiss to happen in the Food Court with a boy who does not even offer her a bite of his pretzel. Kiya would get a good laugh out of that---Kiya has been kissing boys for a whole year! She even frenches!

"Maybe it's not a lost cause," she begins.

"Ki, bestest friend in the world, do not continue to set me up with Jo-Jo, the dogfaced boy!"

"Don't you mean doll faced?" Kiya corrects, believing Jo-Jo is the hottest boy in high school.

"Maybe you ought to hook up with the 'dollface'---that dollface is actually pretty scary coming at you in the Mall!"

"Shelby, you know the rule; you had first dibs on Jo-Jo. Therefore, he is yours forevermore!"

"I relinquish custody---have at him!" Shelby insists.

"Seriously?" Kiya's curiosity is piqued.

"Please---enjoy him."

"No, I mean---*seriously*?"

"Take him with my blessing!"

"What if you change your mind tomorrow?"

"Rest assured, that will not happen. Jo-Jo is a free agent!"

"He wouldn't look twice at me," she says, sadly.

"Why not—you're adorable!"

"I'm fat! Jo-Jo doesn't like fat chicks, he told me!"

"He what?!"

"He didn't technically call me a fat chick but gave me the once over like I was the one he was talking about." She feels depressed.

"If I knew that; I wouldn't have given him a minute of my time! No one calls my bestie names!"

"It's okay; he probably didn't mean it."

"Never-speak-to-that-jerk-again!" Shelby says through gritted teeth.

"But Shel…"

"I mean it. If you do, I'll give him a piece of my mind!"

"Don't ruin it for me, Shelby---maybe I have a chance."

"No—no chance, Ki. You are too good for that piece of crap!"

Kiya gives her friend a weak smile, reluctantly promising to ignore Jo-Jo for all time.

CHAPTER 7

Honoree

"So Shel, whatcha got going next Saturday night?" Deke asks.

"Nice use of the English language, dad."

"Shelby you have become a literary snob since you started high school and began writing for the school newspaper."

"Sorry dad, you shouldn't have read me all those classics when I was growing up."

"Easy to blame dear old dad, isn't it? That's okay; that's why they invented fathers-- to bear the burdens of their children's scorn."

"I appreciate it, dad," Shelby acknowledges, heading for her room.

"No, wait---what about Saturday night? I have this thing, being honored or something. I'd like you to go as my date."

"Oh seriously, dad? I thought you were joking me."

"Saturday night, the Governor's Club and the actual Governor will be presenting my award."

"Award for what, dad?"

"For Outstanding Public Servant, whatever that means," Deke says modestly.

"It means you're amazing, dad. I would love to go---do I get a new dress?"

"Is it essential?"

"Absolutely!"

"In that case, you better get one! I'm sure Kiya will help you choose the best one---very formal. No denim and fringe, no jeggings," Deke jokes.

"Yeah, those are my style alright."

"Remind me, I'll leave my charge card."

"Whoopee!"

"Uh—no Whoopee!"

"Just yanking your chain, dad."

Deke figures Shelby will be the loveliest girl at the dinner but he is not prepared as his grown-up looking daughter descends the stairs. She is wearing a scarlet, strapless dress with a poufy skirt that extenuates a tiny waist. Blonde hair curled around her bare shoulders, settling on more than ample breasts. Deke's heart aches looking at this young version of Marissa.

"You are stunning, Shel!"

"Thanks dad—I've never been stunning before!"

"You remind me so much of your mom."

"Really? Do I look like her? She was so pretty; I could never look that good."

"But you do, honey. I'm so proud to have you on my arm tonight."

"Grandma was pleased you decided to take me instead of your...."

"I can fill in the blank, Shel---nice way for a grandma to talk to a child!"

"But I don't look like a child tonight, right dad?"

"You sure don't! You look like a smashing young lady."

"Smashing and stunning? I'm gonna get a big head."

"It's a beautiful head, Shelby---are you ready to go?"

"Can't wait to meet the Gov."

"Honestly? If that's true, I've been remiss in your upbringing."

"Gotcha, dad!"

Shelby and her father make a fine looking couple and get lots of appreciative glances as they are seated at their table. Deke knows everyone at the table and introduces Shelby all around. They chat and sip on drinks while they wait for the proceedings to begin. On this night of nights, Shelby, almost grown, does not order the beloved kiddie cocktail. She sips on sprite; hoping people will assume its vodka or sparkling wine.

Looking round the glimmering ballroom and the festive guests, Deke's eyes land on another luscious lady! Cress is seated two tables over with her crew from the State Journal. Why he is so surprised, he doesn't know—she is after all, a journalist of the highest degree.

She is animated, talking to her colleagues, smiling at people passing her table. Deke wills her to look at him and as if by telepathy, she turns her head to their table. Sparkling green eyes widen when she sees Deke and a smile lights up her exquisite face.

"Who is that, dad?" Shelby asks, noticing the direction of her dads attention.

"Where?"

"Right there, dad—that hot girl in the black dress."

"Over there?"

"Yeah dad—over there, the one you're staring at."

"Was I staring?"

"Dad!"

"Oh, that's Cress Manchild—she's a reporter for the State Journal. Very talented."

"At what, dad?"

"What do you mean by that, Shelby?" He asks, turning his attention to his date.

"Dad, is that the woman grandma accused you of dating? She said her name was Cress! Coincidence?"

"No actually, Cress and I were having a lunchtime interview when your grandma had her meltdown. It was quite embarrassing for all."

"Do you like her, dad? It seems like you like her."

"Very much; she's a nice girl and always gives me a fair shake in the press."

"In that case, I like her if you like her!"

That's my girl," Deke says, kissing Shelby's cheek.

A few republicans warm up the audience for the appearance of the Governor. To Deke, it is just so much bull! They are laying claim to some pretty wonderful things while Wisconsin sinks to dead last in job creation, among other things.

Finally the 'promise-maker' takes the stage. The lines are drawn; his fans are standing. Most democrats are not.

"Should we stand, dad? Give the governor a standing ovation?" Shelby asks, with a twinkle in her eye.

"I think not."

The Governor reiterates his tired old agenda and the audience listens politely. No one is enthralled. He is not the speaker the President was at the

Capitol Press Corps Dinner, in Washington, earlier in the year. Obama had them chuckling, right from the palm of his hand; Walker is barely holding on by his fingertips. To a fashion, between campaign plugs, Walker honors the press that often brutalizes him.

Presentations are made; Deke is honored, and many from the State Journal get honorable mentions to include his very own, Cress! Is that what she is, he wonders? He sort of likes the sound of it although there are many things which need to be tweaked before he can tell her so!

Everyone is anxious to begin the dancing and end the listening. Tables are cleared and finally rearranged to make a dance floor. On the dais, a string quartet sets up and begins tuning their instruments.

"That could be you up there, someday, Shel."

"Unlikely, dad. I only play to relax."

"It's something to fall back on," he offers.

"I don't plan on falling at all." She says with the confidence of youth.

"No honey, you will not fall. You will achieve all that you desire. You will be successful and wildly happy!"

"Thanks, dad—I hope you're right."

"Guaranteed! Feel like 'tripping the light fantastic'?"

"I'm not sure but I wouldn't mind dancing." She smiles.

"C'mon, clever girl---let's show them how the Allison's do it!"

Shelby takes her father's extended hand. He leads the young 'princess' to the dance floor and feels very proud as he looks down at her. How did that teeny tiny baby turn into such a lovely young lady? He wishes he could ask Marissa that question. Tonight, he feels especially close to his deceased wife.

After a dance or two, Deke guides Shelby over to Cress's table. She has been on the dance floor tonight, as well but Deke doesn't know with whom. They interrupt their dance to stop at her table.

"Hello, Cress," he says softly. Love shines in his eyes and Cress is able to recognize it.

"Speaker Allison," she says, politely. "Congratulations!"

"For?"

"Well, you are an honoree but I really wanted to congratulate you on having the loveliest date here."

"Thank you." Shelby replies.

"You're right, Cress—she's a looker. I'd like you to meet Shelby, my beautiful daughter. Shelby, Cress."

"Nice to meet you," they say at the exact same moment. Everyone chuckles and Deke and Shelby continue their trip around the dance floor. Each time around, his eyes connect with Cress's and crinkle with pleasure.

"Dad," Shelby ventures. "Would you like to ask Cress to dance?"

"Oh no, honey—it's not like that. We're just friends."

"I know," she says trustingly. "I'm just getting tired. I feel like sitting for awhile."

"Are you sure? Won't you feel awkward over there with all those strangers, Shel?"

"No, dad. I'm a big girl."

With Shelby parked at the table, Deke is free to go to Cress, something he aches to do. She looks panic stricken when he approaches her.

"Miss Manchild?"

"Mr. Speaker?"

"My daughter has given me permission to dance with someone closer to my own age. Can I twirl you around a bit?"

"Do you think that's wise, Deke?" she whispers, looking at her colleagues---all press people!

"I got permission from a highest power, that's good enough for me."

Almost giddy, Cress takes his hand and allows herself to be led to the dance floor. If people are watching, if they are gossiping, they don't notice—they only have eyes for each other. Deke holds her a respectable distance away, swishing her around the dance floor. Without realizing it, they are drawn closer and closer until they are touching. Cress can smell Deke's after shave, she sees the start of five o' clock shadow, but mostly she gazes into eyes that never leave her face.

"What a miracle Deke Allison is!" she thinks, joyfully.

With a modicum of jealousy, Shelby watches her dad's expression when he looks at Cress. There is no doubt in her mind that her dad has a soft spot for this reporter. Deke has always been a good judge of character and Shelby trusts his instincts implicitly. Winded, Deke rejoins her.

"Were you bored to tears?"

"No, dad. You looked like you were having fun."

"I guess."

As the night wore on, Shelby tired. Deke was more than happy to take her home. With a backward glance at Cress, they made their way to the valet.

"Fun night," he says, when they are driving home. "Thanks for going along, Shelby."

"It was my pleasure, dad—it really was."

"Well, you dazzled them honey."

"Thanks, dad. You were not too shabby yourself."

Andy is asleep on the couch when they arrive home.

"I'm sorry, Mr. Allison," Netta, their housekeeper explains. "Andy was trying to wait up."

"No problem, Netta," Deke says, hiking the small boy over his shoulder. "Thanks for staying with him."

"Thanks, Netta," Shelby says, dying to get out of her heels.

Much later, as they wait for sleep to embrace them, Deke and Shelby both think about Cress. Shelby is unsure if she has the right to be jealous of this striking woman--she hates the idea of sharing her daddy. Still, if she can bring happiness to her dad, he deserves it. He's been alone a long time; almost four long years!

Deke marvels at how natural it felt to dance with Cress, even in front of all those people. Once her small body made contact with his; he felt complete somehow. Corny as it sounds, Cress is the peanut butter to his jelly. He knows he is treading on thin, thin ice on many different levels.

"What are you, Deke?" he asks himself. "About 18? At Woodstock? Karma and all that jazz? Peanut butter and jelly---are you kidding me?"

He tries to settle down but is unsuccessful until he imagines Cress in some form of undress, placing her hands on him, calling his name. He dozes off with her in his head and about half a chubby.

CHAPTER 8

Busted!

*B*efore he has an opportunity to read the morning paper, he is inundated by phone calls and not the least is his former mother-in-law, Elise.

"Yes, Elise," he says with forced patience. "What can I do you for?"

"Maybe you can explain why your face is spread all over the paper---not dancing with your beautiful daughter who was probably moping on the sidelines while daddy played footsie with his mistress!"

"What the hell are you talking about? Shelby and I danced nearly every dance!"

"Nearly is the operative word, Deke! What would Marissa think of you now?!" she hissed.

"Marissa would be proud at how I am raising her children, Elise. I am certain of that. As for me; I didn't die that day and she would not want me to live like I had!"

"How dare you!"

"No, how dare you! Instead of helping the children adjust to life without their mother, you expect them to live like they died that day, as well."

"That's a lie, Deke! I am trying to help raise them they way Marissa would have!"

"Your memory is short, Elise. You and Marissa never agreed on how to raise her children."

"You're lying and you know it---Marissa and I agreed on everything."

When Deke does not respond, Elise backtracks. "Not when she was a teenager, of course. What parent gets along with their teenager? Even you and Shelby do not always agree."

"It seems when we don't, it's because of some farfetched idea you've place in her head."

"I suppose the picture on the front page of the Capitol Times was one of my farfetched ideas?"

"I haven't seen the newspaper this morning, Elise but I intend to. I will say good bye now so I can see it before the kids come down."

"Try explaining that embarrassing photo away, Deke!" Click!

Deke runs a hand over his face; he's a bit prickly he notices although he's already shaved. Blowing on his coffee, Deke opens the morning paper. The entire front page is a collage of photos from last night's festivities. Near the middle of the page is a small photo of him and Cress, dancing. Next to it is a photo of the Governor dancing with someone other than his wife---Deke's photo is no more or no less scandalous than the Governors. If he is not mistaken, there is a tiny picture in the corner of him and Shelby dancing, as well. Apparently Elise missed that one!

Her intent, as of late, is to discredit Deke but he's not sure why. It wasn't always that way. For fifteen years, Deke had the distinction of being Elise's favorite son-in-law. Of course, he was her only son-in-law but they had always gotten along famously. When Marissa died, Elise's heart broke and crumbled until it finally disintegrated. Deke only wishes she would put as much effort into Shelby and Andy as she does trying to discredit him; they could use the affection of a female family member. Marissa always claimed her mother was a hard-ass!

"Morning dad," Shelby said, sitting down for a quick breakfast.

"So honey, you made the papers," he said, handing it over for her perusal.

"I did?" Squinting, she looked over the front page. "I see you and the reporter lady…oh there we are, dad!" she said, happily.

"I hear they're all jealous up on the hill, Shel."

"Jealous of what, dad?"

"I was lucky enough to dance with the two hottest girls in the joint!"

"Well, Mr. Lucky---I've got to go. Good thing my friends never look at the newspaper…"

"Why---are embarrassed to be out with your old man?"

"Well---yeah, dad! Of course!"

Deke chuckles as Shelby runs out to catch her ride. "She's not traumatized, Elise," he whispers. Andy skids into the room, wearing only one shoe.

"New style, Andy?"

"Huh?"

"One shoe on, one shoe off?"

"No, dad! I can't find my other shoe!"

"Did you look under the bed?"

"I looked everywhere, daddy! I'm gonna be late for school!"

"Then, I guess we better find it," Deke says, leaving his breakfast behind.

Upstairs, Andy throws his covers on the floor and dumps his toy box. "Where is it?"

"We'll find it, buddy. It's not like someone broke in only to steal one sneaker."

"Then where is it, dad?"

Deke bends down and looks, one more time, under the bed. Going down on one knee, he captures a wayward sneaker and holds it up.

"Look familiar?" he asks.

"I looked, dad! I really did---it wasn't there!"

"It's dark under there, Andy---no big deal."

"No dad---it wasn't there when I looked!"

"So, maybe we have leprechauns around here, playing tricks on us?"

Andy is in no mood to be joked out of his funk---he is afraid of being late and is just plain annoyed. "Just never mind, dad."

"In that case, tie that rascal up and we'll get going!"

Deke drops Andy off at the elementary school on his way into the city. He's unable to pick him up from school, but this is one of their housekeeper's duties---that and a healthy afternoon snack!

"It's like you were made to make news," Dan Angus says, perching on the corner of Cress's desk.

"So—here we go..."

"What? No, I mean it---great picture of you and the Speaker."

"But..."

"No but, I wish it had been our front page."

"Maybe instead of frolicking at the party, you might have covered it for the Journal," Cress suggests. "How come they zeroed in on us; the Governor was dancing, as well."

"Yeah, I shoulda thought of covering the event myself …but I was there, in living color; I saw it all!"

"Eye witness."

"Exactly and the things you see when people think no one is watching!"

"Such as?"

"Such as a look; a faraway look, between lovers. A touch that may seem innocent. Secrets whispered on a dance floor."

"I think you're in the wrong business, Dan—you ought to be writing romance novels or at least, writing for the National Enquirer!"

"No, I'm good. Here's today's assignment and I trust you won't find it too objectionable."

Cress looks at the proffered paper. "You want me to interview Speaker of the House, Deacon Allison? Would that be the same Deacon Allison we've interviewed at least thirty times?"

"One and the same."

"Honestly Dan, what questions are left to ask?"

"Make it personal, will ya?"

"No."

"I don't mean personal between you and him—I mean what it's like to raise a family when you're a politician—a widowed politician."

"Have Chelsea do it."

"No Cress, you are the woman for the job—he trusts you and he likes you. Like-likes."

"Are you having fifth grade flashbacks, Dan? This is a bogus assignment and you know it!"

"The voters want to know, Cress. They want to know how an eligible bachelor juggles it all---career, kids, romance."

"As far as we know, the speaker hasn't had romance in his life for a very long time and he doesn't seem to be looking."

"Oh, he's looking alright," Dan assures her.

"He's never seen squiring women about town; he's not into Madison's nightlife. I say he's still mourning."

"I'm calling bullshit on that one, Cress but we won't know till you write up the interview, will we?"

Cress stands and excuses herself from his unsavory company. "You're a dick."

"Just get that interview and write the damn story!" He says sourly.

Outside, on the square, Cress calls through to Deke's private line. If he is busy or in a meeting, he doesn't answer and Cress gets the message.

"Are you free at all today, Deke?"

"Not the best time."

"Has that blasted picture caused a furor in your life?"

"Oddly, very little."

"Didn't Elise see it?"

"Oh, yes indeed. First thing this morning."

"The kids?"

"Shelby took it in stride; she handled it a lot better than her grandma did."

"Thank God for small favors. What about your colleagues? Your staff?"

"Not a word."

"In that case, you are faring better than I."

"Someone giving you a hard time, honey?" he whispers.

"Dan thinks he's got it all figured out, trying to push my buttons."

"Maybe I ought to give your boss a call?"

"That would only confirm his suspicions."

"Screw him."

"I believe I'll pass."

"Certainly relieved to hear that. I wish I could see you today."

"Long lunch hour perhaps?"

"We're working through lunch, unfortunately."

"Could you pencil me in tomorrow; I'd love to spend some time with you."

"Tomorrow looks a helluva lot more promising than today --- if we get our work done today."

"Let me leave you to it then."

"Until tomorrow, beautiful."

Squatting on a bench provided by the city of Madison, Cress wonders how to get out of the asinine assignment Dan has her working on. She wonders if she should be trying to get out of the illicit affair she and Deke share, as well. She doesn't want to let him go but is it fair to him, to his kids, and even to herself, she wonders.

Each day, each time they meet, she feels herself falling more deeply in love with the Speaker. She knows, too, that this relationship can only bring heart break. Deke may be taken with her at the moment but he's a man who falls in love but once in a lifetime. His great love was Marissa—end of story. Even so, she is giddy at the prospect of seeing him tomorrow!

"You are a woman without convictions," she scolds herself.

Tonight she will dream of Deke. In her fantasy, she will listen as he speaks his love for his children and his government. She will taste succulent lips, savor his breath on her face, and will take delight in his tantalizing tongue. Every curve, each gully of his hard, honed body is memorized. Recollections of granite-like abs that skate across hers, of intense erections wielded like an artist might wield their tools: rakes and brushes, spatulas and palettes. Reminiscences so vivid, she literally quakes with desire.

"Dear God," she whispers in the dark. "Please allow me one more day that I might spend it with the man I love. Then, I will come peaceably."

CHAPTER 9

What If?

Cress welcomes the day; it is as though the sunshine is a sign that she is meant to have one more blissful day with Deke. She rises early and tidies up so her apartment will welcome him, as will she.

After her shower, she slips into filmy panties and a matching bra---ruby red in color. She spritzes cologne in each intimate nook and slides her clothing over her hips. An easy access sundress that will not steal treasured seconds away from their lovemaking. She is weak, imagining their noontime liaison.

But first, she must confront Dan Angus and his ridiculous assignment. Dan whistles when she enters his office. Cress is ready for battle.

"Damn, girl—you sure pretty up the place."

"Whatev…" she says skeptically.

"Seriously, Cress, you look good enough to eat!"

"You understand the guidelines for sexual harassment, right?"

"Since when is giving a well deserved compliment considered sexual harassment?"

"Never mind all that, Dan—I want to talk to you about this bogus assignment."

"What's bogus about it? It's a legitimate assignment and I expect you to do it. I want to see something by noon Friday."

"Deke Allison is a busy legislator; I may not even get an appointment by Friday!"

"Oh, I think he'll make time for you, Cress," comes the innuendo.

"I'm not flipping Barbara Walters, Dan----no one is interested in Deke's private life!"

"I disagree! Just do it, write it, and get it back to me!"

Cress feels the crunch; squished between that rock and that hard place. She is fuming when she leaves Dan's office—she does not want to impose on Deke's friendship to get an interview; especially a weak, 'fluff' interview! Her job, as she sees it, is to report the news---not dig around looking for some sort of scandal.

Promptly at noon, Deke knocks on her door. He is greeted with a smile and a warm friendly kiss.

"You look amazing!" He says, taking in the sundress, shoulder length sun singed hair, and delectable moist lips.

"So do you!"

"I want to ravage you all day long but I'm on a schedule; besides I want to talk."

Cressida leads him to a chair and climbs on his lap when he sits. "Are you sure you want to talk, Deke?" she asks, kissing his lips, his cheeks, his eyelids.

Deke's response is immediate and he kisses her deeply, hands on either side of her face. As tongues entwine, Deke's hands slide to her shoulders and finally, to her breasts! The elastic top is malleable and Deke is able to pull it down until he is confronted with remarkable breasts, draped in red. Rosy nubs stand straight out and Deke kisses each one. Cress groans and wiggles on his lap.

Deke rearranges her seating arrangement until she is facing him, legs on either side of his lap. Cress is so compliant, so willing, he forgets his determination to merely talk today. Her skirt slides up until Deke can detect filmy red panties peeking out at him. Effortlessly, he pulls the sundress over her head and presses her hips to his erection. Encouraged by his apparent arousal, Cress grinds into his lap.

Dipping his hand inside sexy panties, Deke finds her damp. He rubs his fingers over her and she arches against skilled fingers. She undulates, awaiting fulfillment. Pulling aside her panties, Deke enters her, straining upward until he fills her many times over. Taking the lead, Cress rises, and then sinks down hard. Hands guide her hips and they move in unison, until they achieve the ultimate in total satisfaction.

Dekes' arms rest at his sides as Cress rests her forehead against this. "This was better than any boring old confab, wasn't it?"

"That it was, sexy girl." Deke agrees. "But eventually talking will be necessary, Cress."

"Why? Are things not perfect?"

"Perfect is exactly the right word but you should have so much more."

"Here it comes," she predicts, "The big kiss-off! Just do me a favor and don't tell me we'll still be friends."

"This is no kiss off, honey. In fact, I think it's time to take it up a notch—you deserve better than a nooner every once in awhile."

"I am happy with any time I get to spend with you, Deke."

"I appreciate that and I feel the same but you ought to have someone who will squire you around the city, someone who is free to take you to events and parties. Someone with a helluva lot less baggage than I've got."

"So, you are dusting me?"

"*Dusting you?* You mean like dumping you? That's the last thing I want to do."

"Then what, Deke? Exactly?"

"I want all of this Cress but more so. I'm not sure if the drama of the situation has me thinking I am in love with you or if, as I suspect, I am falling in love with you. I want to find out for sure."

"Deke, you're still in love with Marissa," she points out.

"Cress Manchild, I will always love Marissa for what we had but that doesn't preclude love between you and I."

"It doesn't? They tell me you are a one-woman man."

"Whoever 'they' are, they are off their rockers---it wasn't Elise, by any chance, was it?"

Cress chuckles at the thought of her and Elise having any sort of conversation. "No, it's the word on the hill—Deke Allison is loyal to the memory of his deceased wife."

"I like to be known as a loyal guy—the thing is; I didn't die four years ago. In fact, I want to live life to the fullest especially now that I've found you."

"Deke," she sighs, kissing him gently.

"I would like to see where this goes—how about you? I would like to date you, in the open, once I've run it by my kids."

"Does that mean you will still go home for dinner every night?"

"It does but once the kids settle down for the night, I can come back. We can go to a late dinner, if you're interested. We can go to the movies or to Jenna's for cosmos. Does any of this sound appealing to you?"

"It all sounds damn appealing!"

"It won't be a walk in the park," he warns. "I don't know how Shelby will take it or how much interfering Elise will do. We'll be hounded by the press…"

"Those bastards! All kidding aside, I would love to give it a try, Deke."

"In that case, after Andy goes to bed, I will speak to Shelby---feel her out. Unless it puts her on suicide watch, we will then schedule a proper date! Are you good with that?"

"You do whatever is in the best interest of your kids, Deke. I'll be around, regardless."

"I want it to be in your best interest too, honey."

"Damn." Cress swore, once Deke returned to work. "I forgot to tell Deke about Dan's stupid story idea!"

Andy is especially animated at dinner. He is downright silly!

"Who wound you up?" Deke asks.

"What's that mean, daddy?"

"Why are you so wild tonight? Too much sugar?"

"Sugar of a different variety, dad." Shelby tells him.

"Meaning?"

"New teacher and according to my brother, 'she's hot!'"

"What does a six year old know about hot?" he grins.

"Dad," Andy says, patiently. "Hot means she's pretty!"

"It does? Hmmmm…I didn't know that."

"And she smells good, dad---like cookies or cupcakes."

"That does sound hot," Deke agrees. "What's her name?"

"Miss Nikki!" he shouts.

"What happened to Miss Sara?"

"She got married, dad and she quit!"

"I see. Now was Miss Sara hot, Andy?"

"Aw, dad! She wasn't hot." The boy is disgusted by how little his daddy knows about life!

"I'm trying to figure out what makes a teacher hot, son."

To demonstrate hot-ness, Andy makes a form with his hands. Instead of an hour glass figure, Andy makes it look like the Michelin man—three rolls instead of two, causing Shelby and Deke to laugh.

"Son, I think you mean like this," Deke shows him what an hour glass figure should look like.

"Ok, daddy," he agrees.

Shelby rolls her eyes; Deke merely laughs at his kids. "Shel," he says, heading in for Andy's story. "Come talk to me before you turn in, will you?"

"Sure, dad—everything okay?"

"Yep, just have an idea I want to run past you."

"Ok, 'night booger face!" She calls to her brother.

"'Night monkey-butt!"

It's a strange night all around. In lieu of a story, Andy wants to talk about his mommy. Deke listens and tries not to interrupt.

"How old was I, daddy, when mommy went away?"

"You must have been about two, two and a half, still a baby really. Why, Andy?"

"Daddy," he says, in all seriousness. "I don't remember mommy. Was she nice?"

"She was very nice and she loved you and Shelby more than anything else in the world!"

"More than you, dad?"

"Yes, more than me but I didn't mind. I knew she loved me too."

"Why'd she go, dad? Why did God take her to heaven?"

"Andy, the easy answer is because he needed her up there in heaven. The hard answer is I just don't know why she had to go when she did because we still needed her here."

"Do you miss mommy, dad?"

"I sure do, son!"

"Me too," Andy says, curling into fetal position on his bed.

"Poor little bugger!" Deke thinks.

After awhile, Shelby comes into Deke's office and sits on a chair across from his desk.

"What's up, dad? I still have homework."

"No rush, Shel—it can wait your homework is done or until tomorrow."

"Tell me now; dad-it will drive me crazy, if you don't."

"It's not a huge deal."

"So---tell me already!"

"Shelby, do you miss your mom?"

"I do—do you?"

"I sure do but sometimes I feel incredibly lonely."

"Dad, you can always talk to me when you feel bad."

"Thanks, honey. Your mom has been gone for four years. I was thinking of asking someone out to dinner—what do you think of that idea, sweetheart?"

"So grandma was right—you do have a girlfriend." She says morosely.

"No girlfriend, Shel. Just someone to go to dinner with, someone to talk to."

"Who is it, dad? That Cress person?"

"Shel, don't say it like it leaves a bad taste in your mouth. She's a wonderful person."

"Would mom have liked her, dad?"

"Your mom would have enjoyed her; she's savvy like your mom was and she's intelligent and she's fun!"

"Can I give you my opinion tomorrow, dad? I don't feel so good."

"Shelby, don't allow this make you feel sick. This is just you and me, talking---I haven't made any decisions."

"'Night, dad." She brushes a tentative kiss across his cheek.

"I love you, Shel."

"I know, dad. I love you back."

At the breakfast table, Shelby won't make eye contact with her dad. He has a very bad feeling about this and wonders if he should have taken Cress's advice and just kept their relationship hush-hush. If the truth were known, Deke hasn't felt such a strong connection with anyone in years—maybe even before Marissa died.

Oh, he'd never have cheated on her or left her but marriages get stale, passion ebbs. It wasn't until she got sick that Deke realized how much she still meant to him. Deke would have happily given his own life to save hers.

"Dad, I've been thinking about what we talked about..."

"I hope you haven't let it upset you, honey."

"It's a quandary, dad," she begins.

"Then forget I ever mentioned it, Shel."

"See, I want you to be happy—I don't want you to be alone," she continues. "Then I think about mom and I wonder if I'm being disloyal to her."

"*You're* not, Shel. If anyone is being disloyal, it is me."

"Not really, dad. You have a right to be happy, just as much as anyone."

"You and Andy give me enough happiness, honey. I am a content man," he lies.

"But not really, dad," the wise teen says. "Anyhow, I'm on board with whatever you decide with this Cress-person."

"You are? Seriously?" This is not how Deke expected this to go.

"Sure. Get a life, dad!" she jokes.

"So you would be comfortable with me inviting Cress to dinner? You know, to meet you and Andy?"

"*Here?*" Shelby looks absolutely stricken.

"It doesn't have to be here, Shel. We could go to a restaurant; I thought you would be more comfortable here."

Pausing, Shelby takes this under advisement. "I think it will be ok, dad."

"Look honey, think about it today, tomorrow, however long it takes for you to feel comfortable with this. I won't invite her till you give me the go-ahead."

"Ok, dad." She agrees.

Andy's arrival at the table ends the conversation. As usual, he is bouncy and creates comic relief. They all leave the house with smiles on their faces.

CHAPTER 10

Explosive Dinner Party

*I*t is decided, with no fanfare whatsoever, that Deke will invite Cress to dinner on Friday night. Deke's next hurdle is Cress herself---she will be reluctant to rock Deke's cozy little dinghy.

"Do it for me, honey," he coaxes.

"Deke, why do this to your kids? They have no desire to meet a complete stranger, wedging her way between them and their dad."

"There is no wedging; hopefully there will be some welding."

"Welding?"

"Uh, melding? You know what I mean."

"I just don't know. I'm scared—what if they hate me? What if they think I'm trying to take you away....or worse, that I'm trying to step in for their mom?"

"I predict they will like you immediately, like I did. I anticipate an enjoyable dinner, no stress, where Andy will delight us all with his antics. They will meet you, you will meet them---no pressure."

"I'll think about it."

"There sure is a lot of thinking going on about a simple little dinner party."

"Dinner party? I thought it was just the family?"

"It is; slip of the tongue. No one but you, me, Shelby, and Andy, the Barbarian!"

Cress smiles at his description of his only son. Based on the stories she's heard, this is a kid she'd like to meet!

"Call me before you head home, is that ok?"

"Of course, whatever you need. Don't over think it, though---it's just dinner."

"No, it's a first impression by the two most important people in your life---hardly just dinner, Deke."

All day, Cress obsesses about what a bad first impression might mean to her relationship with Deke. She didn't mean to fall in love with the Speaker and yet, she has! If his kids come to hate her and her intrusion into their lives, Deke will surely cut her adrift! How her heart would ache, how the tears would flow, how deeply depression would claim her. Even now, tears threaten to fall; just thinking about a life without Deke in it.

Promptly at five, walking from his office, through the rotunda, Deke calls her, as instructed.

"Just heading home, honey," he informs.

"I could set my clock by you!"

"I'm a creature of habit---what can I say?"

"Not a bad thing at all."

"So, what's the verdict---will you be our guest Friday night? We'd love to have you."

"I'd love to have you!" she says, hoping to divert his attention.

"Right back at you but you're just buying time. *Do you need more time?* They're just kids, Cress—nothing to be afraid of."

"On the contrary, Mr. Speaker! Constituents don't scare me, the cops don't scare me, and public opinion means very little to me but your children scare the hell out of me! If they don't like me, my goose is cooked."

"Your goose is alive and well; nothing will change that."

"Seriously, Deke? Even if they hate my guts?"

"Even in that unlikely event."

"Seriously?"

"Swear to God!"

"What's on the menu for Friday?"

"I'm not sure; shall I call the housekeeper?"

"Yes, and tell her to set the table for four."

"That's my girl!"

His words make Cress smile and she hopes like Hell the kids can tolerate her for one measly dinner. What does one wear when meeting 'his kids', she wonders? Hair up or hair down? Lots of decisions go into making this critical dinner a reality.

When Friday arrives and Deke is standing at her door, Cress is literally trembling. If Deke notices, he doesn't say anything---there is nothing worse than being told to calm down when there is so much that can go wrong! She relaxes as Deke keeps her entertained all the way back to Stoughton.

"I could have driven myself, saved you a trip back to the city."

"That would make me a pretty crappy boyfriend, wouldn't it?"

"Not at all."

"Yes, it would, Cress. I'm not that guy---I hope."

"You are the best man I've ever had."

"You deserve nothing less, my love."

"My love? Did Deke just call her his love?" she wonders in awe.

"This is the Speakers Street," he announces like a nerdy tour guide.

"Page Street?"

"That would be the one. This is the Speakers driveway," he goes on to say.

"It's a dandy," she compliments.

"Thank you, my dear! That porch light right there?"

Cress nods, enjoying his game.

"That means welcome---it's for our lovely guest."

"Thank you and thank you for your generous invitation. Thank you for letting me meet your children."

"No, thank you!" He says, as the front door bursts open, revealing a small fireball---presumably Andy. "Here goes nothin'!" Deke says, coming round to open her door.

Andy barrels up to them, peeking shyly at Cress. "Daddy, we're having company!"

"We are?"

"Yep, Shelby told me!"

"Are you sure?"

"Yep, Shelby told me and grandma after school."

"Grandma was here?" Deke is now the nervous one.

"Yep, and she's pissed!"

"What did you say, Andy?"

"I think he said grandma's pissed," Cress whispers, not realizing the relevance of this information.

"Dad, grandma said she's pissed. I'm not saying the bad word—I'm just repeating it."

"That will be enough repeating---grandma shouldn't be talking that way in front of you."

"That's what Shel said! She said to never say the bad word. Oops! I forgot."

"I'll tend to grandma later."

"Ok but she's …"

"Don't say it Andy," Deke warns the precocious six year old.

"I wasn't gonna! But who's our company?"

"Do you see this lovely lady standing next to me, Andy? This is my friend, Cress, and she is our dinner guest."

Peeking at Cress, he smiles. "I'm glad you're not the Governor."

"Me, too! I'm just Cress—nice to finally meet you."

Deke walks ahead with Andy and Cress lagging behind. He has a burning in his gut from the knowledge that his former mother-in-law knows Cress is coming here tonight. Shelby meets them in the foyer.

"Hi dad," she says, giving him one her famous non-kiss kisses.

"Hi babe. Shelby, I think you remember my friend, Cress Manchild? Cress, Shelby."

Very urbanely, the girls shake hands and smile tentatively at one another.

"Welcome," Shelby graciously states.

"Thank you; something smells divine."

"It smells like Netta's pork chops to me," Deke says a bit too heartily.

"Dad, its fried chicken!" Andy scolds.

"I was only off by a sniff!"

"You were off by a helluva lot more than that, Deacon Allison!" Elise erupts through the open door.

"Elise, we are not having any of this right now." Deke says firmly.

"Right here, right now!" she screeches. "I can't believe you would bring your whore into my daughter's home! In front of my daughter's children!"

"Time for you to leave, Elise!"

"I leave when I am damn good and ready!"

"I hope you're ready because you are definitely leaving!" Protectively, Deke blocks her from Cress.

"This is low, even for you, Deke! Look what you're doing to my grandchildren!"

"What I'm doing? Take a look at their faces, Elise—they think you've gone stark raving mad!"

"You look at their faces, Deke---what do you see? I see Marissa's face and still you bring your whore into her home!"

"You have two options, the way I see it. You can apologize and leave peaceably or you can leave in shame when the police get here."

"You bastard—throwing me out of my own child's house!"

"Daddy," Andy says, clutching Deke's arm. "Please don't throw my grandma out!"

Cress finds she cannot move, not even when Elise attacks her, virtually spitting in her face! "You will never take the place of my daughter! You will never live in her home! You will never be mother to her children---the kids know who their mother is!"

"No, ma'am, I am not trying to take Marissa's place..."

"Don't you dare say her name! Don't you say my daughter's name!"

Firmly but gently, Deke edges Elise towards the door. The damage is done: their dinner ruined, the children shaken, Cress mortified! A broken woman; Elise leaves more quietly than she came. The sight of the childless woman breaks Cress's heart and she finds she cannot hate her attacker.

"Grandma's right!" Shelby storms, stoked by her grandma's attack on Cress. "This is my mother's house—you don't belong here!"

She flys into her bedroom with Andy on her heels. "You're not my mommy!" he shouts, scooting after Shelby.

In a daze, Cress backs up to the door. The havoc wreaked here tonight is almost unfathomable. She needs to get away---immediately.

"Cress, honey," Deke implores.

"Please don't say anything, Deke. I need to go home."

Taking her elbow, Deke gently leads her to his car. It is an effort to remain quiet but honestly, he thinks, what is there to say? She will never believe this will pass, may even be forgotten and forgiven—not now. The long quiet ride is almost therapeutic as they both finally let out the breath they have been holding for the past half hour.

Cress will not allow Deke to walk her in. "Go home to your kids, Deke--- they need you now."

"Are you okay, honey?"

"I will be," she promises.

When he leans in for a kiss, she averts her face. That burning in Deke's gut has become a full blown volcano! At home he gets the same treatment from Shelby, who will not unlock her door.

"Andy is sleeping with me!" Her voice so muffled, Deke knows she has been crying.

"Is that what you want to do, Andy?"

"Daddy, I'm sleeping with Shelby—just this once! Did our company leave?"

"Oh yeah, she left." Deke says, figuring Cress is gone forever. He decides he may as well try to read since there will be no sleep for him tonight.

Cress paces the floor, not even trying to lie down. Over and over, she admonishes herself, "What have I done to those children, what have I done to those children, what have I done to those children?" Her guilt permeates the small apartment. Her one consolation? She will add no more stress to their lives because she will never see Deke again! She will do that for Deke and she will do it for his children but if her heart continues to beat in her chest, it will be a miracle!

CHAPTER 11

Amends Required

$\mathscr{S}$aturday morning is a quiet affair at the Allison household. When the children are forced from Shelby's room due to hunger, they keep their eyes averted from their father. He does not try to engage, is in fact, still dumbfounded by the way things have worked out! His efforts to reach Cress have been unsuccessful and his children both look wounded from their grandmother's outburst. Could this have been avoided? Possibly, if he had warned Shelby not to tell her grandma about their dinner guest but he is tired of tip toeing around his mother-in-law.

"Shel, why *did* you tell your grandma about Cress coming to dinner?"

"Dad!"

"I'm not assigning blame; I'm merely curious---how did it fit into a conversation?"

"Grandma called me to talk the way she usually does,"

"You mean to rant and rave?"

"Yes, but she's old so I just listen...I don't mind. She's been on the subject of your---you know the word she uses, dad?"

"I do, go on..."

"I mentioned that I'd met her at the awards and she seemed nice. I said I would find out for sure when she came to dinner. I didn't mean to tell, dad!"

"You did nothing wrong, honey. I'm just curious."

"When she found out she was coming here for dinner, she went absolutely out of her mind---bonkers, dad!"

"We all saw an unpleasant version of that, didn't we?"

"I'm so sorry, dad—I know you wanted us all to get along."

"That's what I was hoping for, Shel." Deke seems like a broken man.

Andy, who has, so far, been quiet, picks this moment to ask, "What is whore anyhow, dad?"

"Andy!" Shelby scowls. "I told you not to ask dad that!"

"I just want to know what whore is! How come nobody won't tell me?"

"It's a bad word, Andy and I don't want to hear you say it again---do you understand?" Deke asks, sternly.

"Yessir!" Andy knows his father's no-nonsense voice.

"Dad, does your friend hate us now?" Shelby asks.

"I have no way of knowing."

"Just call her, daddy. Tell we're sorry," Andy suggests.

"Working on it, son but I'll handle this. You worry about those bad words that keep flying out of your mouth lately."

"OK, daddy—may I be excused?"

"Of course. I'm not mad at you guys—your grandma interfered, making us all slightly nuts. I try not to forget that your grandma lost her only child; you are all that's left of that child. We must cut her some slack but what she did last night was over the top. Unforgivable."

"Will Cress understand, dad?"

"I hope so but remember this; no one takes your place---no one! Your mom would not have wanted us to stay locked in grief. You, Andy, and I did not pass away four years ago---she would want us to live productive, happy lives. We must not be bitter like your grandma."

Shelby went to the head of the table to be closer to her dad. She slipped an arm around his shoulders. "I want you to be happy too, dad."

"Thanks, Shel," he says, patting her arm. "So, what's up for Saturday, Andy? The Y?"

"Daddy, can I just watch cartoons and play my game?"

Deke can see everyone is wasted from the emotional ride they took the night before. "Let's just lay low then. One hour of cartoons, one hour of video games, Andy---choose wisely."

Inside Deke is itching to pound on Cress's door, demanding to be let in! He wants to explain what happened does not mean his kids hate her; they just got caught up in the spell their goofy grandma wove. He is determined to beg for another chance---beyond that, it's up to Cress!

Does she love him enough to give them a second chance? Does she love him, period? She hasn't said but neither has he…but he does! Life will lose its sparkle without her. She liberated his glow, his buoyancy---it will be a tragedy if she is the one to extinguish it, as well.

Cressida Eleni Manchild allows herself twenty-four hours to wallow; more time would be self indulgent! She does everything the romance novels describe as normal break-up behavior. She cries until she hiccups, she throws things, but just a few---no point in trashing her stuff just because her heart is trashed!

She does not, for one second, consider suicide but she does want to run far away from her troubles, from her loss. For losing Deke, although inevitable, is the greatest loss of her life! She remembers his warmth, his humor, his mouth on hers. Deke is a gentleman, a rare commodity in these times. How empty life has become---literally overnight!

Monday morning, she springs out of bed, determined to be the best damn reporter in Madison, Wisconsin! She stalks into Dan's office, hell bent on reaching her goal!

"Aren't you the early-bird? Did you finish that Allison story?"

"No."

"I told you I wanted it by Friday, Cress—it is now Monday! I gave you a day extra!"

"Listen, Dan, I need some time away from the 'hill'. I'm stale, I need a change."

"What's the deal? They all like you up there and they're receptive to you, some more than others," he adds snidely.

"There will be no more Speaker of the Assembly stories coming from me---that's final!"

"So—that's how it is, huh?"

"Dan, you're a gossip monger, actually worse than a little old lady! What about the Children's Museum? Let me work that story!"

"You'd be so much more useful on the hill, Cress."

"I am taking a hiatus from the hill; deal with it."

"Any chance you'll tell me what caused this upheaval?"

"None."

"That's what I figured. Ok, there is a board meeting tonight, 7:00, Monona Terrace. This is when they decide if the city will take over maintenance of the museum. Get that story! Dig deep!"

"I always do. Thanks."

Cress goes immediately to the library where she sets up her laptop and delves deeply into the history of The Children's Museum. It is a mainstay in Madison but is having financial troubles. If the city is willing to jump in, Madison can retain this popular attraction.

She immerses herself in work; anything to keep thoughts of Deke at bay. Her phone has been off for nearly twenty-four hours. Afraid she'll be tempted to read them, she deletes all fifteen messages. They were there, but now they're gone—much like her love affair with Deke. Only now, their beautiful love affair, their affection, their intimacy is tinged with something ugly---guilt! Guilt of tarnishing the memory of the mother of two young children! Guilt for adding to the grief of an unbalanced mother!

She and Deke never imagined they would do this much harm when they picked up the reins of passion. That's how it started: a flirtation, something fun and steamy---how had it gotten so out of hand? Cress, of course, knew the answer; she and Deke had fallen in love! Something beautiful, something sacred, gone sadly awry....

Even throughout the Dane County Board meeting, Deke invades her consciousness. "Go away!" she silently begs. She concentrates on what is being said and takes vociferous notes. When she gets home, she plans to write the hell out of this story---she will do her best to turn something dry into something people want to read. That will take a few hours of writing and editing before once again, she is faced with an empty bed and a shattered heart. Someone said "Love is a battlefield"---how right they were! She is not doing it again, not ever!

Trudging home with her laptop and a deli sandwich, Cress is surprised to find a bouquet of flowers on her doorstep. She knows from where they came but still reaches for the card, which will no doubt, contribute to the millions of incisions on her tattered heart.

It's not from Deke! It's from Shelby and Andy---oh no, why did she have to read it? It read: Dinners usually aren't so hectic at our house---please give us another chance. It is signed by Shelby and Andy and she idly wonders how long Deke held that gun to their heads? How unlike him to use his children to get her back.

She cradles the flowers but only for a moment; she imagines she is holding Deke and takes momentary solace in the illusion. Laying them on the counter---should they stay or should they go---she sets up her laptop and opens her sandwich. She is not surprised when she hears urgent knocking on her door---of course, he will want to talk but she can't, not yet anyhow.

"Cress, please open the door. I know you're in there, the flowers are gone. I only want to apologize. Please let me in."

Cress is almost undone by the sadness in his voice—is it possible he is hurting as much as she is? She has no time to enlist the advice of Dear Abby so she wings it and cowers in her apartment. The banging continues, but she can tell he is tiring. There is a noise that almost sounds like someone sliding down her door---is Deke sitting on her doorstep? What if the Speaker is seen, moping on her doorstep like some kind of pathetic loser? She swings open the door, almost toppling Deke where he sits.

"Hi honey," he says, with a lopsided and thoroughly engaging grin.

"Deke, you can't sit there. Just go home; I'll call you in a few days."

"Is this the big kiss-off?" he asks, using her words against her.

"Do we have to do this right now? I have a story to write, you have kids at home, my horoscope says it's a bad day for serious conversations."

"Mine says it's a bad day to break up with someone you love."

"You read your horoscope? Wait, did you say I'm someone you love?"

"You knew that though—didn't you?"

"No, not for sure. I was hoping and then, I wasn't."

Deke takes a chair and runs his hands over a wearied face. "First an apology is in order. My children have never been cruel before; their grandma wound them up like tops and they are both very sorry for their unkind, if prompted, words."

"No Deke, children and drunks tell the truth. They are just not ready for you to have someone in your life."

"Shelby says they are."

"Really? She didn't sound like it last night. Maybe I'm just the wrong person. Maybe if you chose someone more like their mother…"

"Cress, I made my choice and I think you owe us another chance."

"I owe you? A bouquet of flowers does not erase the trauma of last night's fiasco."

"For any of us. Just try it again, give us a chance to make it up to you."

"Oh God no! I have enough guilt without anyone trying to make it up to me! I can't do it, Deke," she states, tears leaking from her eyes.

"How can you give up so easily?" Deke asks, heading for the door.

"Easy? This is not easy! This is the hardest thing I've ever done but your kids don't need this kind of hassle."

"I'll worry about my kids, Cress. I've been doing it awhile, you know."

"Good. Now go home and do it!"

Inside, Cress wishes Deke would kiss her goodbye; just one more kiss, one more embrace so she can breathe again. Losing Deke is tantamount to losing oxygen.

CHAPTER 12

Coping...

The days pass but the doldrums do not; the ache of loss is deep. Her story is an unmitigated success; an emotional plea so that the children of Madison get to keep and enjoy the innovative Children's Museum. Some say it is her article that tipped the scales in favor of supporting the museum. The city ultimately takes over the care of the museum. Her head does not swell but she is proud of any influence her story may have had. Mostly, she is relieved the museum will be there for the next generation of children.

Deke is so proud of her story and its influence; he sends a note to congratulate her. That benign little note vibrates through the arteries of her heart and she is even sadder than before. She actually smells it to see if his scent is on the generic note card. Gently, she places it in a drawer but refers to it often; just to stay close to him.

Deke's schedule does not vary. He is home every night by six for dinner with the kids. He gives an uninspired version of a bedtime story to Andy each night. His renditions do not contain the humor they once did---no weird voices or sounds, no joking, no fun!

"Daddy, talk like the ox; you always talk funny when you're the ox!"

"I do?"

"Daddy, I'm tired. I don't need a story tonight." The disappointed little boy tells him.

"Andy—we always read a story! It's our thing."

Andy does not know how to explain it to his dad; he's no dang fun anymore! He reads in a monotone. Kermit the Frog may have been Speaker of the Assembly Deke Allison for all the variety in pitch Deke offers! As a storyteller, Deke is not himself.

"I know, I'm just tired."

"Okay, buddy---is everything else ok? School okay? Do you need new underwear or anything?"

Andy giggles at his dad's feeble joke; at least he is trying to be the old, fun Deke! "Undewear's ok, dad."

"Not crawling up your hiney?"

Going along with an old joke, Andy pretends to check his bottom. "No, not right now."

"That's good; I don't want to see any picking!"

Andy chuckles. When he was a little guy, he had a bad habit of pulling at his butt. Deke likes to remind him of that when they are joking around and no one else is in the room. He appreciates his dad's efforts; he knows he doesn't feel so good.

"Ok, good night, buddy! Love ya!"

"Love ya!" Andy says, accepting a noisy kiss on the cheek.

On the way to his home office, Deke taps on Shelby's door.

"Everything ok, Shel?" he asks through the closed door.

"I'm ok, dad—just doing homework!"

"Okay honey. If you need me, I'll be in my office."

"Alright, dad. 'Night!"

"'Night honey."

As Deke makes his way to the office, Shelby explains the situation to Kiya---secure and happy Kiya; a girl with two parents, no siblings, and everything she desires.

"You mean he actually has a girlfriend?"

"I guess so. He brought her to dinner. Grandma said the whore was his girlfriend!"

"She actually said that---the whore?"

"I know—queer, right?"

"Very. What's the big deal---why shouldn't your dad have a girlfriend?"

"I don't know, Ki. To grandma, it's huge deal."

"Why? Your mom has been gone a long time, Shel. No offense."

"None taken. My mom was my grandma's only child; she still can't believe she's gone!"

"Four years later? Are you kidding me?"

"Ki, you've never lost someone you loved, have you?"

"No but seriously, how long can this mourning go on?"

Shelby whispers, "It never goes away!"

"I'm sorry, Shel—I didn't know you were having trouble with this, too."

"Not every minute of every day but I do think of her every day. I still miss my mom."

"So, you didn't want your dad to work it out with his whore?" Kiya just likes saying the word.

"I don't know—you should see him now. He's so sad, it breaks my heart. I think he really loves her."

"Your dad loves a whore?"

"Enough already! I'm sure my dad would not fall in love with a whore! Those are grandma's words…"

"And we all know grandma is a whack!"

"Exactly. I better go; I still have to write my article for the paper."

"Oh, that's right, you are an esteemed reporter for the Citation!"

"And don't you dare forget it," Shelby jokes.

"I won't. Can't wait to see what you do with that African display---can you say caribou?"

Laughing, she pushes disconnect. For an entire hour, she sits before an empty word document. How to start? Too bad Cress didn't stick around; she might have asked her---reporter to reporter! Dad will suffice, she decides.

"Dad, are you busy?" He doesn't look busy but he definitely seems down; he has no enthusiasm for life since Cress ousted him from her life.

"Never too busy for you, honey."

"I have this article to write for the Citation but I don't know how to get started…"

For a moment, Deke seems especially broken, obviously thinking about Cress and her writing career. Shelby pulls a chair close to her father.

"Are you okay dad?"

"Not quite okay, buttercup but working on it."

"I'm sorry, dad. I wish I could make this right for you, wish I could take back the words that sent grandma off the deep end. Please forgive me."

"It's not your fault, Shel. Your grandma went round the bend four years ago, not just last week. She'll be the same in twenty years; nothing will help to prepare her for another woman in your life. Her heart cracked wide open as did ours."

"But we moved on, didn't we dad?"

"I'd like to believe we did, honey, but I'm not so sure. Did I spring this on you and Andy too fast?"

"I'm not sure. It came as a shock but your sadness is what hurts us now."

"Then, I better brighten up!"

"Don't brighten up for us, dad---feel better for yourself."

"You're a wise woman, Shelby Allison---now let's work on a beginning for this article!"

Shelby explained the African display, complete with animals, to her dad. At first, he was stumped, wishing he could call Cress for advice but of course, she was incommunicado!

"You want to attract attention to your work."

"How do I do that?"

"One surefire way is to ask a question, engage the reader." Deke says, remembering a hundred college essays.

"Like what?"

"What—do you want me to write if for you, too?" he jokes.

"That would be helpful."

"I want to be helpful but I've done all the homework I'm ever going to do."

"That's ok. I think I got this. Thanks, dad!" She kisses her dad on the cheek.

Once she comes up with a compelling question, it's all downhill for Shelby and the article almost writes itself. Kiya gave her the idea. She writes: "Have you ever seen a caribou, up close and personal? How about an antelope?"

In bed, Shelby's attention turns to her father; a man who has lost his zest for life. How do they retrieve it? If only Cress would answer his calls! Shelby wonders if she is hurting as bad as Deke is?

Before bed, Deke persistently puts in another call to Cress. When had she become so important to him, he wonders, listening to the ringing of his unanswered call. On her end, Cress is luckier than her former lover—her phone is turned off so she won't be tempted to answer it. She is sleeping like a log, thanks to recently prescribed sleeping pills. She only wishes she could take them round the clock!

With Kiya's help, Shelby has a plan to resurrect the relationship. She cannot bear to see her father so unhappy. She and Kiya plan to go downtown to the Journal office to find Cress and to talk some sense into her! Ideally then, if she really loves Deke, she will pick up the blasted phone!

It takes some fancy footwork on their part. First they have to come up with bus fare; Kiya is always loaded so that works itself out. They need an alibi for where they will be; they sure as heck cannot say they are going into the city! There is always the old standby; Kiya is at Shelby's and Shelby is at Kiya's.

"But what if we go to all this trouble, find the newspaper office, and she's not there, out on a story or something?"

"Damn, I didn't think of that. You'll have to call her, actually set up an appointment."

"I can't call her—what if she calls my dad?"

"She's not calling at all. I don't think she'll call him."

"Then why would she agree to see me?" Shelby asks the million dollar question.

"You're Deke's kid! Of course, she'll see Deke's kid!"

"Why?"

"She'll be curious, for one thing. She'll also want to make sure he's ok. It's so obvious, Shel!"

"I'm sorry, Kiya, but I'm not allowed to read romance novels. I haven't got this all figured out yet."

"It's a pity; I've learned a helluva from Harlequin."

"You've taught me a lot from Harlequin," Shelby agrees with a smile---it isn't *technically* reading, is it, if Ki reads it to her?

"Alright—if this will help my dad, I'll make an appointment."

"With his whore?" Kiya giggles.

"Sometimes I wonder why I confide in you," Shelby says with disgust.

"Just joking, sista! Besides that whore might be your step mom someday!"

"Please stop saying "whore"!"

"Gotcha!" Kiya knows when Shelby is serious.

With nervous fingers, Shelby calls the Journal and asks to speak to Cress Manchild.

"Miss Manchild is on another line, may I ask whose calling?"

"Could you tell her it's Shelby?" As well known as her father is, Shelby does not want to use their last name.

"Please hold."

"I'm on hold," she tells Kiya. Her hands are sweating and it's hard to hold the cell phone. "What do I do if she tells me to take a hike?"

"I dunno but I'll take that hike with you!"

"Gee, thanks."

"Hello?" Cress sounds as scared as Shelby feels.

"Uh, hi Cress, this is Shelby. Shelby Allison. Deke's daughter?"

"Hi Shelby. What can I do for you?" She isn't sure if the kid called to chew her ass again or if Deke has put her up to this or what?!

"I'm coming in to the city tomorrow after school---me and Kiya. I was wondering if I could stop by and talk to you."

"Shelby, your dad didn't put you up to this, did he?"

"Oh no—my dad has no idea I'm calling you! I swear!"

"I didn't think this was Deke's style but I had to ask. What's this all about then?"

"It's uh, girl talk." Shelby stammers.

"Girl talk?"

"Yeah," Shelby says, giving Kiya a thumbs-up.

"What time will you be here?" Cress is definitely wary.

"Could we stop by at 4:30?"

"I guess I could arrange to be here at 4:30. I'm on the fourth floor."

"Thanks so much, Cress."

"See you tomorrow," she says softly, realizing she is talking to Deke's lovely offspring!

Shelby and Kiya congratulate themselves on their most excellent plan with high fives all round—except there's only the two of them.

"Told ya!" Kiya yelps.

"You were right, Ki—all that smut reading has certainly paid off!"

"My mom says every book has something to offer—she wasn't kidding!"

"So, do you have enough money for our bus ticket?"

"And then, some."

"Supa! Thanks Ki—it's a good plan."

"What are you going to say to her when you are face-to-face with…"

"Don't say it, Ki!" Shelby puts up a warning finger.

"I wasn't going to, just fooling around," Kiya laughs.

"I'm gonna feel her out, see if she really and truly loves my dad."

"How will you know?"

"You're the reader of romance, Kiya---you tell me!"

"Hey, it's your turn to come up with a great idea. I've been carrying you all day!"

"True, that," Shelby agrees. "I think I'll be able to tell."

"Shelby, have you ever talked to anyone who is truly in love?"

"Only you----when you're looking in the mirror!"

"Real funny."

"Thanks."

"I was being sarcastic."

"I know."

"So alright, tomorrow after school, we board the bus for Mad City. We head over to the Journal where we will pick the brain of your father's lady love! Haha—you thought I was gonna call her your dad's whore, didn't you?"

"Kiya—so help me God, I will kill you if you keep saying that! It's bad enough I have to hear my grandma talk like that; it's just plain mean!"

"Is your gram still spouting obscenities?"

"Only day and night! Like Cress, I sometimes don't answer my phone."

"What can be done about her? She's turning everyone against her."

"I know, right? I tell her that but she continues her rant until I say good bye."

"It's weird."

"I think I'm going to tell her not to call me anymore unless she talks nice about my dad. She acts like he is a total dirtball and has had forty women since my mom left."

"We all know that's not true."

"Everyone but grandma." Shelby shakes her head in disgust.

"She used to be so nice; when we were little."

"Something broke in her head when my mom passed away—she's never been the same. It's sad really."

"Well, I'm sad because I have a ton of homework so I'm leaving."

"Need help?"

"Naw. Hey good job on that African article; I see you got a byline."

"My first byline! It feels so good! I'll have to remember to show my dad, he gave me a hand with it."

CHAPTER 13

Guess Who's Coming to Dinner?

Cress is on pins and needles all day, awaiting her appointment with Deke's oldest child---what can Shelby possibly want? If she wants Cress to scram, they've already made that abundantly clear! If she wants to exact her pound of flesh, Cress will leave her to it. Maybe it's no more or no less than a school assignment? Tour the newspaper? That would be Cress's best case scenario. A light tapping on the door tells her she does not have long to wait!

Cress has to smile as the two shy girls enter her office; they don't look like they want to rip her ta-ta's off!

"Hi girls," she says, indicating to chairs in front of her desk.

"Hi Cress," Shelby begins, sitting on the edge of her chair. "Thanks for seeing us."

"Of course," Cress manages, seeing Deke's daughter has the same people skills he has! "What can I do for you?"

"I wanted to apologize for that big scene at our house."

"Not necessary, Shelby---it must have been a terrible shock to you all."

"No, it really wasn't. Dad gave us the option. If we had said no, he would have taken us all to a restaurant."

Cress felt some relief in knowing that.

"When I told grandma, it just sort of slipped out. I had no idea she would flip out like that."

"Understandable; don't worry about it, Shelby."

"Then when she started acting so goofy, we all got in on it---it was pure insanity and I am so sorry for whatever mean thing I said to you! I don't even know what poison came out of my mouth!"

Tired of being quiet for so long, Kiya chimes in, "Everyone feels really bad, Miss Manchild---especially Mr. Allison!"

Shelby gives Kiya a sidelong glare. She shrugs, feeling properly chastised.

"Please forgive me and Andy, too!"

"Nothing to forgive, Shelby---its ancient history."

"But it doesn't have to be, does it? I mean, couldn't we all start all over again---except grandma? We'd all really love that."

"I so appreciate this visit and I know your heart is in the right place but this is something between Deke and me."

"But you won't talk to him—how can he fix it when you won't talk to him?"

"Maybe it's not fixable. Your family is still grieving; I should never, ever have interfered with that."

"Cress, you're wrong. That was just grandma firing us all up. Dad and Andy and I are ready to explore our options."

Cress could scarcely contain a smile. What a sweet, sweet child.

"And you haven't even asked about my dad! He's heartbroken and you haven't even asked about him!" Shelby stands, ready to bolt!

"Shelby it's all I've thought of, looking at you. I'm afraid any actual mention of Deke will rip my guts out, leaving them to lie on the carpet in front of you and Kiya." Tears well up in her eyes, tears she prays will not spill in front of these innocent children.

"If you love my dad, you will give him an opportunity to explain!" Shelby storms out of the office with Kiya close behind. Through her tears, Cress can see that Shelby is crying, as well.

"Brave young lady," she thinks, trying to suture her guts back in.

Shelby cries all the way back to Stoughton. This does not turn out to be the adventure she and Kiya hoped for!

"Shel, are you ok?" Kiya asks, over and over.

Shelby nods but continues to weep. "She doesn't even love my dad!" she says, gasping for breath.

"I don't know, she was crying when we left."

"Was she?"

"Bawling, just like you are now."

"But what's it mean? Maybe she was crying because we interrupted her afternoon massage!"

"Huh?"

"I don't know. I just want a happy dad! Why'd he ever have to meet her anyhow?"

"Maybe so he can experience love one more time?" Kiya offers.

"You're so good at this, Ki. You could write those romance novels you like to read."

"Yeah?"

"Definitely. Now tell me what to do about my dad."

"Let him work it out, Shel---he's the grown up."

"Kiya, my dad hasn't read any of those novels; he doesn't know how these things work."

"He's pretty smart though."

"But is smart enough?"

"I don't know. They say if you're really smart, you'll never fall in love."

"Dammit!" Shelby swears.

Kiya stays for dinner and notices the changes in Deke immediately! He doesn't tease her like he usually does; there is no playful joking either. Even Andy is subdued around him now.

"Got your homework done, girls?"

"Dad, its summer vacay. I told you that."

"That's right," he says. "Are you spending the night, Kiya?"

"Is that okay, Mr. Allison?"

"That's what's done during summer vacation, right?"

The girls look at one another and shrug. Shelby can't wait to be excused so she can get Kiya's take on her dad's behavior.

"Who is that man and what has he done with Speaker Allison?" Kiya asks when they are sequestered in Shelby's room.

"See what I mean?" Shelby seems on the verge of more tears. Kiya doesn't know how to help her bestie.

On the twelfth day of self imposed isolation from Deke and his children, at the third bleating of her phone, Cress picks up! Her heart takes on a calypso beat and her hands perspire because caller I-d indicates it's Deke on the other end.

"Hello?" she says in a tiny voice; afraid if she speaks too loudly, he will disappear.

"Thank God---Cress! Thank you for finally picking up!"

"I shouldn't have."

"Of course you should have—it is not every day the Speaker of the Assembly calls!" he jokes.

"Actually, it is every day," she corrects, a small grin cracking the determination in her face.

"I was afraid you would pick up on that," he jokes.

"What do you need, Deke?"

"There's that reporter in you, cutting to the chase, brooking no nonsense!"

"Uh, Deke?"

"Cress, please let me come by so we can talk."

"If you come by, there will be no talking—you know that, Deke."

"Then meet me in a public place."

"What's the point? We gave it a shot, it wasn't enough."

"There was no shot, Cress---the mission was aborted when Grandma Crazy showed up, spilling her filth!"

"Your kids deserve better, Deke."

"There is no better for me, Cress. I love you; I want you in my life."

"*For what?* Sex is easy to come by. I'm sure you've had other offers along the way."

"Cress, my kids keep me grounded, I need that. But honey, you made my life fun for the first time in a very long time! If you think this is all about a roll in the sack, you don't know me very well!"

"White Horse Inn, 12:30."

"Got it."

Deke knew this was his final chance with Cress; he didn't want to blow it! He whistled as he walked to the restaurant; it was the first happy sound coming from his body in two weeks! Cress is seated at what they had come to think of as 'their table'—a discreet little table-for-two in the corner.

She is as beautiful as he remembers. She offers up a tentative smile although she feels her heart might burst with the joy of seeing him!

"Hello beautiful," he says, taking her hand as soon as he sits down.

"Deke," she blushes.

"Thank you for coming."

"Probably shouldn't have," she murmurs.

"Cress, of course you should have! We love one another, we should be together."

"Deke, when there are little people involved, love is not the only factor."

"Love is all there is. I don't know if love is an easy thing for you to come by but for me, it's only happened twice. I feel fortunate to have experienced love that many times---how about you?"

"How about Shelby and Andy, don't they get a vote?"

"Of course they do. They cast their vote two weeks ago when they agreed to invite you to dinner. What happened after that was not on them; that was the work of a woman unbalanced by her grief."

"I know."

"Don't penalize the kids and me for what Elise did — please. It would be unfair."

"Deke, what do you expect now? I met with you; I listened to what you had to say---now what?"

"Now you come home with me to dinner."

"What? No."

"Why not, honey? It's the right thing to do."

"I don't know if it's right for me, Deke. I may be all grown up but I'm feeling mighty vulnerable right now."

"Of course, you are---you were a victim the other night too. We all were. Now we must be proactive, must not allow Elise to win! Come to dinner, baby."

"Did you run this by the kids?"

"We'll surprise them."

"Not a good idea!"

"You're right, it's not a good idea---it's a great idea. They'll love it."

"Yeah, sure they will. What's for dinner?"

"Does it matter?"

"It does if it's liver."

"It's never liver."

"Pick me up before you leave town at 5:15."

"At your place?"

"Unless I wise up and decide to stick around the bar all afternoon."

"I'll collect you at your place unless you tell me different. Thanks, Cress."

Deke does the most wonderful and unexpected thing; he leans in and kisses Cress on the lips---right in the middle of the White Horse Inn! After she recovers from his public display of affection, she goes back to work.

"Well, if it isn't Mrs. Allison back from lunch," Dan sputters.

"Give me a break." Cress walks past him as though he is inconsequential.

"The Speaker is getting awfully bold," he continues.

"If you don't like his politics, try voting him out."

"It's not his politics I am referring to."

"Seriously Dan, I don't care."

"You'll care when that sweet good bye kiss goes viral on Youtube."

"What! Are you tailing me? How'd you know about that?"

"Jesus Cress, do you think you and Deke are the only people who lunch at the White Horse? Kate was at the bar when it happened. Snapped a picture and she was not the only one!"

"Who else?!" Cress demands.

"Who the hell knows, the place was packed."

Cress lowers herself onto her chair. "What next?" she mutters.

"You better warn lover-boy! Maybe suggest he keeps himself in check until you are alone."

"Why do you care, Dan? All it makes is a better story for you."

"I'm not that big a jerk," he announces. "Not all the time anyhow."

"I'll be the judge of that."

Cress dials Deke's number but it goes directly to voice mail. She sincerely hopes she can reach him before they have their liaison splashed across the front page of the opponent's newspaper! Even if she can, it won't stop the inevitable.

"What will Elise make of this?" she muses.

Cressida does not make contact with Deke until he picks her up at her apartment at 5:15. She realizes panicking will not solve the problem; it is what it is. Much as she would love Deke to come up for awhile, she knows he adheres to a strict schedule so that he is home for dinner every night.

"Hi honey," he says, leaning in for another kiss.

Cress looks around to see who might be watching or worse yet, snapping photos.

"Deke…"

"I've heard all about it and I don't give a damn! I'm a grown man and I've mourned long enough—let the pieces fall where they may."

Cress smiles at this assertive Deacon Allison---this is the attitude that got him so far in politics and made her fall in love with him.

"I was just thinking about the kids…"

"I don't think we've given those kids enough credit. They're resilient and they're smart and they both have empathy; I think they'll be okay."

Cress didn't tell him she knew Shelby was onboard with the relationship---she was sworn to secrecy. "What about Elise?"

"I feel for her, I really do but I can't live my life vying for her approval. As long as Marissa remains dead, Elise will have a hard-on for me. In her mind, I should have been the one with cancer and Marissa should have been the survivor."

"It's kind of over-the-top."

"I know and I can only hope she'll get some help; some grief counseling."

"Do you see that happening?"

"I really don't but I will have to check her if she keeps upsetting my kids. I don't want to---they're her lifeline, but they don't need to be involved in her craziness."

"What do they think about her histrionics? Has she done this before?"

"Not exactly like *this* but I've never been involved with anyone before. She's put some of her goofy thoughts into their heads and it's got to stop. Shelby loves her 'old' grandma so she's polite to the new, crazy one."

"Do you think she'll be dropping in tonight based on the picture?"

"I doubt it but if she does, she won't get past the front door. I confiscated the key Marissa gave her for emergencies."

"That must have been a humdinger of a confab."

"You have no idea." Deke says it all by rolling his eyes dramatically.

They are scarcely in the driveway when Andy barrels out the door to greet his father. "Daddy!"

"Hi bud," Deke says, lifting him high in the air.

"Hi Andy" Cress says, stepping out of the car.

"Oh-oh!" Andy says with eyes wide and almost frightened.

"No oh-oh, Andy. Mind your manners and say hello."

"Hello," he says in a small squeaky voice.

"Now run in and tell Netta there will be four for dinner, please."

"I see you warned the troops," Cress says under her breath.

"Are you kidding and chance a repeat of our last effort?"

"Good point."

Inside the foyer, Shelby waits to greet them. Although this is what she hoped for, she is still shy.

"Hi Cress," she says warmly. "Welcome."

"Thank you," Cress demurs.

"Let's go inside and visit," Deke says, throwing a comforting arm around her shoulders. "It's time my girls got to know one another."

Shelby does not know what to make of all this. Her dad is certainly jovial and that's what she wants but this show of affection between him and Cress is a bit unnerving. Guiltily she thinks of her mother but cannot find the bitterness her grandma feels.

"Cress, what can I get you to drink?" she politely asks.

"Honey, I'll uncork a bottle of wine for us—why don't you get a drink for you and Andy?"

"Sure, dad." When she comes back, she has young Andy in tow. He sort of hides behind his sister until she sits down across from Cress. He scoots in beside her and looks at the floor; he is feeling shy. Cress is a beautiful lady; even a little boy can see that.

"Andy, why so shy?" Deke has the poor taste to ask the wriggling little boy.

"I'm just tired."

"How does a six year old boy, on summer vacation, get tired?"

Cress and Shelby give Deke the stink-eye which he reads loud and clear.

"Oh," Deke says. "We'll try to get out story in early tonight. Ok?"

Let off the hook, out of range of his father's scrutiny, Andy's head bobs up and down in agreement.

"Uh, not to give bad news or anything, dad..." Shelby begins.

"Let me guess—your grandma has been ringing the phone off its hook?"

"How'd you know?"

"Cress and I had lunch at the White Horse Inn today and someone took a picture which they are spreading all over town and the internet. You heard it from me so be prepared."

"What's off the hook, daddy?" Andy asks.

Everyone looks at Andy, not understanding his question.

"Off the chain?" Shelby asks, referring to the popular phrase among teens.

"Daddy said off-the-hook."

Deke is still puzzled.

"You said 'ringing the phone off the hook'" Cress remembers.

"Of course! That shows how old daddy is---in the old days, our phones hung up on a hook. When they rang, we took it off the hook." Deke explains.

Andy thinks about Shelby's smartphone and wonders how they would hang it on a hook. Deke knows his bright child is trying to comprehend the concept and gives him a hand.

"Phones used to be big and bulky, son. They had a part to talk into and it was sort of shaped like a hook. I'll try to find a picture of one online later, ok?"

"My great-aunt Katie still has one. She's used it for over fifty five years," Cress volunteers.

"No kidding—rotary dial and all?"

"Yep, it's cool—she'll never trade it in."

"I'd like to see one again."

"I'd take you over but she'd kind of growly and touchy about that phone. She's afraid someone will break it after all these years."

"There might be something to that; its' not like she can replace it."

"Is she old, Cress?" Andy asks.

"Very."

"How come old ladies are so grouchy, dad?"

"I don't know, son—I think their feet hurt."

Mulling this information over, Andy shakes his head.

Dinner is quiet, uneventful, and delicious. Baked chicken and noodles with alfredo sauce; Cress compliments Netta who blushes in appreciation. Andy seems to be wearing a lot of his sauce.

"This is better, isn't it?" Deke asks everyone assembled at the table. It is unanimous; it doesn't take grandma long to wreck a party, they seem to be thinking. Precisely at that moment, Shelby's phone shrilly rings.

"Oh gosh, speak of the devil---its grandma."

"Are you done eating honey?"

"Yeah, dad."

"Maybe take that call in the other room?"

"Do I have to take it, dad? She just keeps saying the same things over and over!"

"I'll grant you, she's annoying but I doubt she's ever ditched you, Shel."

"You're right."

Cress is surprised Shelby doesn't talk back and doesn't argue with her father; she just does the right thing! Unusual behavior for a teen these days.

CHAPTER 14

A Tentative Peace

"Would you girls mind keeping one another company while I read Andy his story? That way I won't have to rush right back," Deke pointedly looks at Cress.

"Sure—wanna watch a movie, Cress?"

"No, no, you don't have to babysit me, Shelby. You do what you would normally do; I'll be fine right here."

"I was hoping we could talk, get to know each other."

"Of course, if you want to but please don't feel obligated."

All the way to his bedroom, Deke and Andy playfully discuss which book they will read tonight. Inside, Cress is hoping they choose a short one; she knows Shelby is just being polite.

"Cress," Shelby begins, "how did you and dad meet?"

"Oh gosh, I have been interviewing your dad for years. Sometimes in his office, sometimes over lunch."

"Was my mom alive when you started interviewing daddy?"

"You know, she was and I think I met her once at your dad's office."

"Seriously?" Shelby is clearly excited.

"If I remember correctly, she dropped in to see your father…and you were with her. I think Andy was a baby. She was sort of frazzled the way moms get and your dad introduced us."

"What did you think of her, Cress?" Shelby is literally sitting on the edge of her seat.

"She was obviously very beautiful, looked a lot like you, and she seemed tender with your dad and you and Andy. This is just a perception from a five minute meeting."

"Were you and daddy in love even back then?" Shelby asks the million dollar question.

"Oh honey, no! Your father is not that kind of man and I could tell he held her in high esteem and loved her very much."

"I didn't know how long…"

"Shelby, your dad did not look at another woman for four years…until a couple of months ago. I was the lucky, lucky woman he picked."

"So, you're in love with my dad, right?"

"I love your dad enough to step back if any of this becomes a problem for you or Andy. I mean that with all my heart and soul."

"You'd give him up?"

"I would and I will, if this is too much for you guys."

"What a nice thing to say, Cress." Shelby says sincerely.

"You and Andy have been through a lot; you're down to one parent and if you decide not to share, I will completely understand."

"For my part, and I know this is business between you and my dad but I would like to get to know you better, see how it goes."

"You're a wise young lady; I'm all for going slow."

In record time, Deke is back!

"Dad, did you actually read him a story?" Shelby asks, not wanting her brother to get cheated because her dad had company.

"It was quick one but it was Andy's choice; seems like he has something on his mind."

"Should I talk to the runt, dad?"

"You could but I think he has to work it out by himself."

"Was it my appearance at the house, Deke that gave Andy so much to think about?" Cress asks on the drive back to Madison.

"He's a little guy, Cress. Life holds lots of questions so I'm not sure what he's thinking."

"If he's, at all, upset…."

"I don't know that he's upset exactly; just trying to come to terms with a new situation. Cress, your heart is in the right place but I would never sacrifice my kids, not even for love. If this becomes a problem, you will be the first to know."

"That's all I ask."

It seems everyone has much to think about and the long ride back is mostly devoid of conversation. Deke and Cress ride in companionable silence until they reach her street. Cress finds herself feeling nervous—will Deke ask to come up or will he hurry back to his children? What if he doesn't? They haven't been together in weeks.

"When you said you didn't have to hurry back, does that mean you can stay awhile?" Her voice sounds husky in the confines of the town car.

"I can't do a slumber party but I sure would like to come up."

"I will send you packing in two hours time!"

"Sounds good but we may have to amend that to two and a half hours. I have missed you so much and we have two weeks to make up for!"

Shivering in anticipation, Cress takes Deke's hand. There is no heated rush when they enter the apartment, no frantic groping, fondling. Theirs has grown into grown-up passion; deliberate, not rushed.

Deke slides his shoes off and lies down on her bed. Standing at the foot of the bed, Cress begins a slow strip tease to the songs of Nickleback; hard, throbbing music to undress by! She unties one shoulder strap of her sundress. Deke cannot take his eyes off her and rolls on his side so he might get a better view. Expecting the dress to fall with the untying of strap two, he is fooled. Her full, round breasts have the power to hold up the silky material. Deke doesn't know where to look; at her hips, rolling with the beat of the music, or at her chest---eventually that has to fall, right?

Impatiently, Deke reaches to the bottom of her sundress and pulls. Full, round bundles of firmness, high on her chest, make him firm! Quickly, Cress slips out of her dress entirely. She climbs into bed in only a thong. Deke makes quick work of that and brushes his hand across her soft little tuft.

"Your turn," she says, licking her lips.

In record time, he sheds his clothing until they are skin-to-skin. Deke's throbbing member is the only thing keeping them at bay. Unable to take her eyes off it, Cress, strokes it gently until he is purring. His hands stay busy as well; exploring her magnificent breasts and the juncture where her legs meet. He finds her wet and willing and slides neatly inside. Cress groans, prompting a quick, satisfying dance.

"Was I too fast?" he asks.

"No---was I?"

"I could hardly wait; you felt so good!"

"It was just what I needed, Deke."

"Me, too---the next time I'll make use of all the bells and whistles. I promise," he says kissing her.

"Not sure I need all that. It was wonderful, Deke."

"Do you know why it's always so great?"

"Why?" she asks with a grin.

"Because I was made to fit perfectly inside you!"

"Oh, I thought you were going to say because we love each other." She sounds disappointed.

"That, my love, goes without saying."

"It can never be said too many times; you know."

"I intend to make it my life's work to never let you forget how much I love you." Deke slides over and gently kisses her.

Cress relaxes in his arms and their kiss deepens. His lips progress down her neck to her delectable shoulders and beyond, until lips are locked onto a nipple. She groans and arches her back; take it all, she seems to be saying. Deke does his best to do that very thing; licking, suckling while his hand squeezes her other breast, lest it feel left out.

His downward trail leads his lips past the washboard abs to the small, but appealing tuft. He buries his nose in the fluff and inhales the womanly smell of his lover. Like a firefly, his tongue flitters inside, and back out again. Cress rises and falls with the darting of his tongue and Deke slides two fingers deep within. Clutching his hair, she is almost undone. Like King Kong, Deke climbs up her writhing body and embeds himself deeply inside her. Each thrust elicits another and another until they come in an exhausted heap.

"Oh man, how I wish I could manage a slumber party tonight."

"Me, too but I understand."

"I would like to awaken to your beautiful face and your warm body, Cress. That would be a dream come true."

"For me, as well."

Deke gently kisses her eyelids, her cheeks, and finally, her mouth. "Somehow I've got to drive my tired old ass back to Stoughton, to make sure all is well at the homestead, check on my youngins."

"What if you slept for two hours, set the alarm, and then drove when you weren't so tired?" Cress offers.

"If I don't go now, I'll never go," he remarks.

"In that case, I'll lock the doors and windows and handcuff you to my bed!"

Chuckling, Deke sits up. "There's no one I'd rather be chained to! No one I'd rather have as my jailer."

"Oh, be careful what you wish for! You did read <u>Misery</u>, didn't you?"

"Saw the movie and now I'm looking at you with a whole new set of eyes---freaked out eyes!"

Cress giggles at the look of mock terror on his face. She walks Deke to the door and thanks him for dinner.

"What about the dessert?" He asks, with a leer.

"Especially nice dessert," she comments. "I could eat that dessert every night."

"I'll see if I can accommodate you."

At the door, they kiss quite awhile until Deke has to drag himself to his car for the long ride home. Exhausted, he drops his briefcase in the foyer and heads up to check on the kids. A note on his pillow, in Shelby's handwriting, warns him that grandma has called three times and is on the warpath.

"What's new?" he shrugs off the warning.

At seven a.m. he finds out exactly what's new as Elise's car skids into the driveway. She is pounding at his door before she even shuts off the ignition. He and the kids are in for drama to accompany their frosted flakes!

Though Shelby let's her grandma in, Deke bars entrance. "These children have to go to school and I am not sending them off upset because you don't know the meaning of decorum!" He states sternly.

"I don't know the meaning of decorum, Deacon? It was not my picture plastered all over the newspaper, kissing another woman!"

"Dad?" Shelby looks at her dad to dispute the charge.

"Look at what you've done! Look at her face; now she's worried sick!" Deke charges.

"She ought to be—her dad is a two timing bastard!" She reaches out like she wants to rake her nails across his face. Deke stays those deadly claws.

"And who am I two timing, Elise? A corpse? Marissa has been gone four God damn years!"

"And that gives you license to go whoring around?"

"I thought you said Cress was the whore, grandma?" Andy asks, coming down to see what the racket is all about.

"Andy, if that word comes out of your mouth ever again, you will be grounded---are you picking up what I'm laying down?"

"Yessir, daddy."

Hearing her small grandson use that word, a word that came directly from her mouth, takes the wind out of Elise's sails. She literally crumbles in the doorway and Deke has to catch her before she falls. She slumps down on the chair and cries bitterly. She is a beaten woman; crushed by a cruel, unfair universe!

"What has become of us?" she sniffles.

"Grandma, are you okay?" Shelby asks, with concern.

"Not yet, honey but I'm gonna be." She pats the small hand on her shoulder.

"Deacon, I know this is not what Marissa would want me to do but I can't seem to help myself. I can't move on like you have; I can't forget my beautiful daughter!"

"Elise, is that what you think I've done? I've never forgotten her. Believe me, I think of Marissa every single day. I remember the wonderful marriage we had; the two amazing children she gave me."

"But Deke, you've found someone new and it won't be long and my daughter will be but a distant memory to you and to the children."

"No grandma, *I promise*. I will never forget my mom," Shelby whispers, tears cascading down her cheeks.

"None of us will forget Marissa but I don't have her here to talk to, to ask advice of, to share the joys of parenting. I have no companion, no lover, no dear friend and I don't think that is how Marissa would want me to live---do you?"

Tiredly, Elise shakes her head in surrender. "I wish I could accept her death but I can't."

"I think grief counseling might be a good idea, Elise. The kids and I could probably use some, as well."

"Deacon, is this something we could do as a family? Dare I hope ---am I still part of your family?"

"It's been a rough four years for us all but we're still a family. These kids need their grandma now more than ever." Deke leans down and hugs his former mother-in-law.

Elise is beyond exhaustion; she can barely stand—life has become such a heavy burden for Marissa's grieving mother.

"I say today, our family needs a mental health day!" Deke announces.

"What's that mean, daddy?"

"It means no school and no work and no more crying! Today we will enjoy a leisurely breakfast *all together* and then, we will relax and regroup. Catch up on our reading or our video games or sleep all day, if you like. Text your friends."

"If only I could sleep," Elise groans.

"You're dead on your feet. After breakfast, I'll take you home. You can rest, knowing we're all good around here. When you call, I'll bring your car over."

"You guys plan how you will spend your free day. I'll order breakfast and call in. Excuse me."

Andy is already battened in at the recliner, playing a video game. Elise pulls Shelby onto the chair next to hers. She holds her young granddaughters hand, remarking how like her mother's it is.

"Grandma, I like it when people tell me I look like my mom. When you start missing her, you call me. Maybe you will feel closer to her when you talk to me."

"Thank you, sweetie. I'll definitely take you up on that."

In his office, after calling his secretary, Deke places a quick call to Cress. He explains the situation and tells her how much he misses her. Exiting his office, he finds Shelby and her grand mom talking quietly, intimately. He can only pray Elise is still not trying to poison his children against him again.

After a big, old fashioned family breakfast, Elise assures Deke she is okay to drive herself home. She does seem stronger almost like a burden has been lifted from frail shoulders. Deke hopes so for the sake of his children who still truly need their grandma.

"I'd feel better if I drove you."

"I'd feel better if you'd stay with the children."

"Will you call us so we know you got home safely?"

"Absolutely, and Deke? I appreciate what you've done for your kids and how you've kept their mother's memory alive. I honestly do."

"I treasure those memories, as well, Elise."

"Thank you and if you can possibly forgive my intrusion into your personal life…"

"We're family and the kids and I have never forgotten that, just like we have never forgotten Marissa. We'll weather this, Elise and become stronger."

"If I can…"

"Tomorrow I'll have my secretary look into to some grief programs so that the whole family might get some closure. It might be helpful for the kids to express their loss to a neutral party."

After Deke does some paper work, after Elise calls to say she's made her way home, after Shelby texts Kiya fourteen times, Deke tells Andy to shut down the video games.

"Awwww, man."

"How about an old fashioned board game, guys?"

Both look blasé about it but since they enjoy time with their father, they agree.

"Can I pick, dad?" Andy asks with renewed interest.

"You pick the first one and Shelby can choose the second."

"We're, uh, playing *two* board games, dad?" She looks nauseous at the prospect.

"We'll see how it goes, honey." Deke says sympathetically, not wanting to force his interests on his kids.

"Let's play Animal Match Game!" Andy shouts.

"Andy," Shelby reminds him. "You're six, not two and a half."

"I know but I'm so good at this," he holds up the preschool game.

"Because you cheat." Shelby chuckles.

"How does one cheat at a board game?" Deke is skeptical.

"Dad, he takes twice as many turns as everyone else and hides the ones he turns over."

"So—Andy, there will be no cheating. Got it?"

"Got it, dad." He has the decency to look sheepish.

The family sits down to the big wooden table and Andy spreads out about eighty cards, all upside down.

"This one game just might take all afternoon," Deke muses.

"It goes really fast, daddy."

"It may not go so fast when you don't cheat," Shelby tells her little love.

"I said I won't cheat!" Andy sits back in his chair, arms crossed, an unusual scowl on his bright freckled face. "Can I go first, daddy?" He asks, brightening.

"You always do." Shelby remarks.

It takes a full hour to turn all those animal pictures over and Deke sort of wishes he'll cheat so it will speed things up a bit.

"Told ya, dad," Shelby says as though she can read Deke's mind.

"I say we finish this game up and take a break---how's that for you, Shel?"

"Merciful!"

When the animals are all counted and returned to their box, Andy is the undeniable winner!

"See, Shel---I didn't even cheat!"

"Yeah right."

"I didn't, did I, daddy?"

"I saw no cheating," Deke verifies. "But I need a cup of coffee and a break."

"I need a rope," Shelby says, indicating a hangman's noose is in order after a long game of animal dominoes.

"Can I watch Sponge Bob, dad?"

"You bet," Deke says, escaping to the kitchen where Netta is cooking dinner. "Smells good," he says, carrying his coffee to his office. Shelby disappears to her room for a well deserved break.

Looking round his office, Deke thinks, "There is peace in our home tonight."

CHAPTER 15

Fare-Thee-Well, My Love

Seeing Elise at the cemetery is not an unusual sight. She is there weekly; sometimes daily. The reason she opens her eyes in the morning, the reason she climbs out of bed is right there; lying in a cold, cold grave. Even after four years, she cries at every visit.

"Well darling," she begins through a deluge of tears, "I came to tell you I can let you go now. I have kept you too long; your place is no longer here with me, with Shelby, or with Andy."

Gulping air, Elise tries to steady her ravaged heart, to gain her equilibrium. It is hopeless and she is forced to sit beside her dearest love for fear of falling in a heap upon her! Tenderly, she pulls weeds and stray grass that has the audacity to grow on Marissa's headstone. Satisfied with the housekeeping, she continues to soliloquize.

"I've been selfish. When you died, I wanted to die and I wanted to take Deke and the children with me…so we could all be together again, on the other side. But Shelby, the spitting image of you, with a mind as quick, has important things to do—she deserves a chance to do them all! And that force to be reckoned with, Mr. Andrew Allison, can conquer the world, if he has a mind to!"

Thinking of Marissa's extraordinary children, Elise is again, overcome with deep and abiding sorrow. What a shame these innocents will not have their mother to guide and protect them! Thank God their father is such a fine human being!

"But you knew that, didn't you, darling? You knew the kind of man you married, the type of father Deke is---that's how you could go away so peacefully. I should have trusted your judgment but I have been bitter; have raged against my Lord for taking my only child!"

Elise searches her pockets for a tissue with no luck. Like an abandoned child, she dabs her nose with her sleeve. It matters so little, she thinks. Snot on one's sleeve; what is that compared to the loss of a child?

"I'm finding I need a little help with this whole thing, my sweet. Deke made me see that. I'm going to see a counselor; not to be able to forget you—just so I can remember about Shelby and Andy. Someday sweet day, they're going to have some questions. They'll ask me about their mommy, and I want to be there to answer them! So you see, darling, I need to stick around and I need to stay strong so I'm there, if your children need me."

"I've kept you too long. Find your peace as I shall find mine. Love you forever!"

Dusting herself off Elise stands, arches her back, and looks at the sparkling bright sunshine. Feeling hopeful for the first time in four years, she makes her way to her car. It's the first time she's left the cemetery without bawling!

Deke wants to ask Cress to lunch but he is behind in his work after his unprecedented day off. He calls, just to hear her voice, just to tell her he misses her. She sounds so down, he is tempted to reschedule his afternoon appointments.

"So, Dan has me investigating domestic abuse cases in Madison."

"For what purpose?"

"He's doing an expose on it in conjunction with a production of the Vagina Monologues."

"The what?"

"Oh Deke, don't tell me that word is offensive to you?"

"Well, it's not like we bandy it around the dinner table at night."

"Maybe you should."

"I'm going to call that a bad idea, Cress."

"I guess it's not a very lovely word although there are worse. But the Monologues are important because they insist violence against women stops!"

"I'm all for that! In fact, I would love to make a contribution. Let's get the word out and let's raise some money to do it---how can I help?"

"In the course of this assignment, I'll find out. We'll all do our share."

"Sounds great! But on a selfish note, when can I see you?"

"What do you have in mind, Mr. Speaker?" She asks in a sultry, sexy tone of voice.

"I propose we put our heads together---and maybe a few other body parts, as well. We'll talk about the very first thing that comes up."

"Where'd you dig up that old line, Deke---second grade?"

"Seventh actually, I was trying to talk dirty to you! Guess it backfired, huh?"

"You could say that but it was a decent effort. Well, not really. Pretty lame, actually."

"Shouldn't you be stroking my ego instead of obliterating it?" He jokes.

"Is it really your ego you would like me to stroke?" Comes her seductive reply. "I was thinking I might stroke something else."

"Aww, man!"

"See Deke, that's how it's done. Sexy Talk, 101."

"I bow to your expertise."

"I love a man who knows when he's *licked*."

"You're killing me and I have a meeting in three and a half minutes! They'll think I'm happy as hell to see them!"

Cress giggles. "Are you free for lunch tomorrow, Mr. Speaker?"

"White Horse Inn?"

"How about my place instead?"

"I could do that! I could definitely do your place!"

"What time can I expect you?"

"12:30?"

"Perfect and Deke, drive over---no point in wasting precious moments on a jaunt!"

"I like the way you think. I like the way you do everything, Cress."

"Right back atcha!"

Deke's evening sails along as he anticipates tomorrow's exciting lunch. The only food he requires is food for the soul and Cress supplies it oh so, well! He can't wait for bedtime so he can begin an exciting brand new day!

The kids seem subdued but not unhappy. Elise has made herself scarce and only stops when invited. Shelby makes sure her grandma gets an invitation to dinner every week. It goes well as does their therapy. Deke suspects the kids were hurt even more than he realized when they lost their mother but it seems like they are on the mend and so is Elise!

Later, in bed, he finds himself talking to the woman who was his best friend for most of his adult life. He feels the need to explain a few things.

"I hope you're watching, honey. I hope you approve of the way I am raising our kids," he whispers. "I want to explain about Cress…I wasn't ever looking for a replacement for you. I couldn't find one even if I was looking—you are one in a million. But the gentleness of this woman is something I've craved for four long years."

Deke realizes there are tears pooling in his ears; he doesn't realize he is softly weeping.

"I thought you would outlive me, Marissa. I thought I'd have a 'grabber' and you would be a sexy widow; men banging relentlessly on the door. I thought until that happened, we would live happily ever after, enjoying our kids and our grandkids. But you bailed on me! If I am to be honest, I was pissed! You didn't even leave any operating instructions! You didn't warn me---*why didn't you warn me?* I hadn't been without you in eighteen years—you should have warned me!"

Deke punches his pillow and flips it on its side---it's unfortunately, flat as a sewer cap.

"So you have an opportunity to make it up to me. You look down upon us and if you think we're doing okay, if you're okay with this thing between me and Cress, just send me some sort of sign. It doesn't have to be the parting of a sea or anything, just a little sign that I will recognize. Love you."

"Love you? Is that what you said?" he questions himself. "How can you love two women at the same time?"

Deke thinks it over and his thoughts travel through eighteen years with Marissa. "I remember when we decided to start a family---the very night Shelby was conceived, in fact. You wanted to make it especially memorable with soft lighting, a bubble bath made for two, and the sexist prim and proper nightie in the world. It was virginal white but it was translucent, leaving little to the imagination. With your alabaster skin, you actually shimmered and I never wanted anything or anyone more!"

Remembering the sight of his wife, looking virginal and hot all at once makes Deke's jockey shorts feel tight and bunchy. "See baby, you've still got it." He whispers.

"As though you were accustomed to stripping for a man, you raised that nightie over your head, with a practiced slowness. Only later, did you admit you had practiced in front of a mirror. To this day, it was one of the hottest displays I've ever seen! Knees followed by thighs followed by the silky, untouched patch! I could not take my eyes from that thatch of hair although presumably, there was the tummy and finally erect nipples staring me in the eyes, tantalizing me!"

Deke presses his erection as though that will make it go away.

"Even now you torture me, my love, my wife. You didn't wait for me to claim you; you came to me, you lay upon my heated body, straddling my manhood. You climbed on top until you sheathed me, damn near strangling me with your tight, inexperienced body. You called out after that first deep lunge but continued to ride me; going deep, rising, going deep until at last, I died 'the small death.'"

"That time, I did not give you satisfaction, I know that, but we got better at pleasing one another each time we met." Deke fidgets with his member, trying to adjust it. He grazes its length and he imagines Marissa riding him like the twenty year old animal Deke was!

"So great," he silently moans. "And you were right; Shelby was created that very night! That was all on you, baby—the way you did it, the way you pleased me, the way you pulled out all the stops!"

Remembering, Deke moves and thrashes in his lonely bed. The memories are too vivid to control. "Marissa…" he sighs, after long self battering minutes…

Recovering, Deke is madder than hell at himself---what is he, about fourteen? "Even at fourteen, you didn't pound your own pud!" he scolds himself. He pulls the pillow over his head and tries to go to sleep despite his embarrassment.

In the morning, Deke remembers his humiliation as he undresses to shower. More scolding until he decides it's all this recent talk about Marissa that made him vulnerable. "Vulnerable? Is that what you're calling it now, you sick bastard?"

So entirely disgusted with last night's behavior, Deke doesn't even wash his member, just lets the water skim over it! Guiltily, his thoughts turn to Cress. "You're a douche," he tells himself. "Later you will be using this unsavory member with her, telling *her* you love her---what kind of dirtbag does that make you?"

In anticipation of that moment, Deke thinks about the beautiful Cress. He is moments away from touching her. He wonders if he should confess his sins but dismisses that thought without serious consideration. It will serve no purpose, he decides. She doesn't have to know she's in love with a deviant.

At 12:33, Cressida is standing in her open doorway, awaiting her lover. She is properly attired, only she knows she has no panties beneath her chaste skirt. It will be a surprise Deke will appreciate.

"You look exactly like a high school girl," he says, noticing the plaid skirt and pristine white blouse, ankle sox, and even penny loafers!

"I know, right? But actually I've got detention."

"I can only guess at the infraction," Deke says, drily.

"I've been a very bad girl."

"In that case, Cressida---what do you think would be an appropriate punishment?" Deke asks, getting into the role.

"Whatever the punishment, it ought to be *hard*."

"No problem there," he agrees, a projectile already in his pants. "Do you need a spanking or shall I ground you?"

"No spanking," she quickly stresses.

"In that case young lady, you're grounded!"

Cress throws herself on her bed and pretends to wail. Lying on her belly, Deke notices her sweet, bare bottom peeking out at him. He quickly sheds his clothing and presses himself into her back. The skirt slides up until it is around her waist and Deke has free access. They slide around a bit and Deke reaches round the front to titillate the squirming woman under him.

Cress lifts her butt a bit and Deke enters from behind, pressing and grinding her into the mattress. He kisses the back of her neck and tries to get close to her ear. His large hands cover hers, on either side of her head, and he drives deeply into her. The sheets, the blanket rub on her front and Deke works his magic from behind. It is almost an overload of pleasure and much as she hates to, Cress releases--like a runaway tsunami.

Deke follows with a resounding grunt. With pleasure this intense, it takes them a moment to recover. Deke does not want to disengage, wondering if it would be possible to lie like this forever.

"Am I too heavy, honey?" He whispers.

"No, you are perfect. Don't move, don't leave me."

"I never will." Deke says solemnly.

Cress lifts her head. "Really, Deke?"

Despite her pleas not to move, Deke slides next to her. She turns to him and they kiss and snuggle.

"Love does not come easy to me, Cress. I thought I was lucky to find it once; I never dreamed true love would come to me twice."

"I was not prepared for this to mean so much either," she admits, crawling deeper into his armpit. "Now what? I don't want to rock your boat, do not want to be a problem for your family, for Shelby and Andy."

"Another reason I am devoted to you; your concern for the welfare of my kids. I love that."

"Of course! How can we be happy if they are miserable? We must go slow."

"Thank you, thank you! That is what I would like to do; let them get used to another woman in their dad's life, let them come to love you as much as I do."

"I'm down with all that, Deke," she agrees.

"So let's start with dinner on Friday night! We'll go out, just us four—well, maybe Kiya too."

"Kiya is Shelby's best friend?"

"You *have* been paying attention," he jokes. "Shel has been begging to go to the Melting Pot---does that suit you, as well?"

"Does it! I've heard it is a long meal but fun all the way!"

"You've never been there either?"

"Not yet; can't wait but listen, if they don't want me along, do not insist---please."

Rising and buttoning back up, Deke knows his lunch hour has exceeded their two hour limit but was it worth it!

"I'll run it by the kids tonight at dinner and get back to you---does that work?"

Sitting up, Cress notices she is at Deke's zipper level. How she would like to take advantage of her proximity to this man's extraordinary staff. As Deke buttons his shirt, Cress runs a hand the full length of him. He shudders and his pants bulge immediately.

"No time, honey," he says, in something of a panic.

"Not even five minutes?" she asks, licking her delectable lips.

"Five minutes?" He weakens, reacting to the unzipping.

"Just five, babe---just five." She promises as she releases the 'beast'. Moistening her lips, she accepts him into her mouth. Deke growls with her manipulations. One small hand cups the area underneath as she licks him from tip to base. Her free hand wraps around the base of his shaft and she works it up, down, in and out. Deke uses her shoulders to steady himself as he makes love to her mouth and finishes this unexpected scenario in just under five minutes!

"You never cease to amaze me," he says, leaning in for a farewell kiss. *"BEST LUNCH EVER!"*

CHAPTER 16

Together But Apart

After another lovely dinner made by their housekeeper, Deke and the kids sit back and chat. No one seems in a hurry to leave the table and Deke enjoys these rare moments of tranquility.

"I've got a joke!" Andy tells them. Shelby does a slight eye roll thing but otherwise, they wait patiently for him to remember his joke. "Ok, how do you catch a unique rabbit?"

Deke and Shelby make a big deal of trying to figure it out. "Got me."

"Unique up on him!" Andy cracks himself up. "How do you catch a tame rabbit?"

"Let me guess…" Shelby says.

"Tame way!" Andy shouts before his sister ruins his punch line.

"That's a good one alright," Deke chuckles.

"But Andy what does unique mean?" Shelby asks.

"I dunno," he admits, "but I think you sneak up on him or sumthin'"

"You figured it out without even knowing what unique means, pretty good, runt!" Shelby congratulates her little brother.

His grin literally goes from ear to ear; nothing is better than approval from Shelby!

"Now you need to tell him what unique means, Shel---for next time."

"Oh yeah," she agrees. "Unique is like you, Andy---you're one of a kind. There is no one like you."

"Nice explanation, Shel."

"I don't get it," he scowls.

"It's a play on words, son. It really means nothing at all but its fun!"

"Did I tell a funny one, dad?"

"It was pretty good," Shelby and Deke agree.

"I gotta go——may I be excused, dad?"

"Of course, but what's the rush?"

"I gotta call Braden and tell him my funny joke!"

"That joke has probably been passed around kindergarten classes for three decades," Deke observes. "None of them get it but they all laugh---now that's funny!"

Shelby and Deke have a good laugh about the unfunny joke and she leaves to text her bestie.

"Shel, before you go, I want to ask you something. I was thinking we haven't been out to dinner in awhile, unless you count Chuck E. Cheese. Friday I would like to take you, Andy, and Cress to the Melting Pot----how does that sound? You could invite Kiya if you want."

"Can I think about it for awhile, dad?"

"Sure. You let me know---are you bothered by my asking Cress?"

"Not exactly but if Kiya is there, I won't be able to talk to Cress—you know how Kiya is. But it will be fun for me if Kiya is there…I'll figure it out, ok?"

"Just let me know so I can give Cress some notice and you can give Ki some notice."

Shelby agrees before disappearing into her room. Deke stays at the table awhile and wonders how people make second marriages and families work? How do families meld together, he wonders? Do they ever really become one? He sure hopes so as he has long term plans for Ms. Manchild.

Friday night goes off without a hitch. Shelby brings Kiya and Deke brings Cress. Shelby places herself between Kiya and Cress so, ideally, she can speak to both. Andy is excited to plunge his chicken chunks and bread into the molten cheese and his nougat into the chocolate. The food is divine but takes hours to consume. They stick around for as long as Andy can sit still.

"So cool, dad," Shelby says.

"It is and the food is scrumptious, that beef is so tender." Cress agrees.

"Takes a helluva long time to eat though," Deke mentions.

"We do this at home all the time," Kiya tells them. "We have one of these pots and the long forks."

"Sounds like a lot of work to me," Deke says.

"But well worth it, Speaker Allison."

"If you say so, Kiya." Deke says, flicking her arm with his fingers.

"This is my first time with fondue," Cress admits.

Shelby smiles at her as if to say, it might be Kiya's first time too. Cress picks up on what she is saying.

"Anyone feel like a walk after dinner?" Deke asks.

Everyone agrees a stroll in downtown Madison will be a good thing. It is a beautiful night and Madison is a safe place to walk at night. They pair up with Kiya and Shelby leading the way and Deke and Cress bringing up the rear, with Andy bouncing everywhere! Occasionally Deke's hand bumps hers and Cress feels close to him although she'd love to be free to hold his hand in public.

After a few blocks, Deke leads them back to the car. Their first drop off is Cress.

"Thanks for letting me tag along," she says to the kids in the backseat.

"Anytime," the forever polite Shelby says.

"Do you think she meant that, Deke?" she asks when he walks her to her door.

"What's that?"

"Shelby said 'anytime'—do you think she means that?"

"I'll find out. She is a polite girl."

"Yeah, that's what I was thinking."

"I better get down there," he says, cutting to the chase. "Although I'd dearly love to come in," he says, leaning in for a kiss.

"I know. Hey, thanks for dinner."

Deke embraces her quickly and leaves. Someday he'll be taking her with him, he thinks with a smile. Having all the people he loves under one roof would be entirely great!

After two more dinners with the family, Deke thinks it's time he and Cress have some alone-time. It is a rare occasion when Deke does not eat dinner with his kids so it is with trepidation; he invites Cress to go to Porta Bella on Saturday night. He explains it to the children over dinner and if he expects a commotion, he is disappointed. They are fine with it and he is almost hurt by their acceptance.

"Like a real date, huh, daddy?" Andy asks.

"I guess. Hey, what do you know about real dates? You're not sneaking around, going out on dates at night, are you?"

Andy laughs so hard, he almost falls off his chair. "Daddy, I'm scared of the dark!"

"So you say."

"Where are you going, dad? Somewhere romantic, I hope?" Shelby asks.

"I'm not sure how romantic Porta Bella is but its dark---does that make it romantic?"

"It sure does. And dad, don't sit across from her, sit next to her---it's more intimate."

"And intimate? That's a good thing?"

"Very. Dad, haven't you ever dated before?" Shelby wrinkles up her nose.

"I dated your mom."

"Way back, dad---things have changed. You're going to have to up your game with Cress."

"Like how?" Deke definitely wants to play his "A" game.

"After a romantic dinner, take her to a dance club."

"Dance club? I don't dance, Shel. You know that."

"You don't have to actually dance, just feel the vibes, dad. Trust me, Cress will dig it---any girl would."

"I will take this all under advisement, maybe run it by Cress."

"No! Dad, don't ask, surprise her. Girls love to be surprised."

"They do?"

At Porta Bella, Deke places himself next to Cress, so close their arms are touching.

"This is cozy," she smiles. How she would love to kiss him in this dark, intimate restaurant.

After a sumptuous Italian dinner, Cress feels like a walk. Before she can suggest it, Deke directs her up a flight of stairs to a dance club---a dance club, for God's sake! The esteemed Speaker of the Assembly at a dance club? Inconceivable!

Deke fetches drinks for them both while Cress looks for a corner to blend into. The lights dazzle and mesmerize her, the beat of the music infiltrates her core, the uninhibited dancers inspire her. She finds herself swaying to the tunes and people- watching. She has never been a dance club kind of girl but...

"What do you think?" Deke asks, handing her a cosmo.

"What?" she shouts.

He waves off his remark, kissing her on the cheek. A table is freed up and they claim it. It is cluttered with empty bottles and glasses and spilled beer or maybe urine. Cress is not sure. She holds onto her glass and sits back a bit.

For an hour, maybe longer, they watch the dancers and drink two cocktails. In all that time, no one clears their table or offers to bring them another beverage. Both times, Deke makes his way to the bar to get their cosmos.

The club pulsates with life and Cress thoroughly enjoys their time there. An hour does it for her and she asks Deke if he is ready to go. He is most definitely ready to go!

"Wow!" he says once they are out in the fresh air.

"I know, right? Wanna take a walk?"

"Do I!"

"What was that all about anyhow, Deke? You don't think I need all that, do you?"

"I don't," he confesses, "but this was Shelby's idea of the perfect date."

"For her or for us?" She grins.

"I'm not sure but the Porta Bella was a good idea, right?"

"Extraordinary, delish! And I loved that you sat right next to me."

"Shel's idea," he confesses.

"It was a good one and the dance club? Totally fun!"

"So, we'll do it again, right?" Deke teases.

"I didn't say that." She laughs.

Deke takes her hand and they walk in companionable silence through streets still bustling with activity in the college town. They turn down State Street and look in the windows of bookstores and consignment shops and trattorias and bars. Everything on this street pulsates with youth, activity, and fun! Street entertainers litter the street and chalk artists display their work. Cress drops one dollar bills into each overturned hat for a tip.

"A patron of the arts, I see." Deke observes.

"I try to do my part," she sighs. "Buy me an ice cream cone?" she asks, outside an ice cream parlor.

"You bet," he agrees. "What flavor?"

"Pistachio."

"And if they don't have that one?"

"They have it," she says confidently.

"Ahh, a frequent shopper?" Deke inquires.

"Something like that," she smiles.

Deke comes out carrying two cones; one pistachio, one chocolate. "The scooper told me to say hi to Cress," he says.

"Thank you!" she says with a smile.

"Old boyfriend?" he feels irritation at the thought of another man.

"It's complicated," is all she will say. Deke is gentleman enough not to press--- that was then, this is now, he thinks.

They sit on an outdoor bench and enjoy their ice cream as the night wears on.

"You should probably take me home pretty quick here," Cress suggests.

"I know but I hate to."

"Do you think you have time to come up?" She asks hopefully.

"Lord knows, I want to but I better get home. The kids will expect a full report."

"I know how you can make it spicy," she entices.

"Probably not tonight, honey but what about Monday, lunch?"

"Real lunch or a nooner?"

"Your choice, of course, although I know what I would like."

"I think I can just about make it till Monday," she agrees.

"Just the promise of it will keep me going the rest of the weekend."

"Me, too. Besides I have a story to write before Monday morning."

"The domestic abuse one? How's that going?"

"To be honest, it's a bitch! You would not believe what goes on right here in Madison, Deke! Pitiful!"

"What can we do? I have a daughter, I have a girlfriend---what can I do, specifically?"

"Awareness is the first step. The old guard still believes domestic abuse is the business of the family and the law shouldn't get involved."

"What is this, 1952?"

"Exactly and while they are relying on the benevolence of husbands and fathers, women are being murdered! Money is needed, lots of money to provide shelters and safe houses for women and their children. Money for education---for men and women. It's an uphill journey and we haven't gotten very far! 1952 is pretty accurate."

"I look forward to your article."

"It won't be purty," she notes.

"All the more reason to expose what's really going on! Right here in this beautiful, evolved city!"

At her door, Cress fights the urge to lure Deke in. She so wants to be with him tonight but there are small people to think of, not just her overactive carnal desires. She chastely kisses him and watches as he descends her stairs.

It takes Cress less than an hour to knock out the final draft of her story. It's a powerful slant on a powerful story. She's pretty proud of it but still bored to tears on a Saturday night! In the past, on nights like this, she would call Eric and then, drop in on him. He would do things guaranteed to make her relax and forget her troubles.

For an instant, Cress wonders what her old pal is up to...

"What kind of person are you?" she scolds. "You say you are in love with Deke but seem willing to toss it out the window for a romp!"

Cress shakes her head; no, no, she will never cheat on Deke! She's never loved anyone the way she loves him—she's just new at this. She curls up in bed with a book and out of sheer boredom, falls asleep.

In the morning before she rolls out, Cress likens her relationship with Deke to one she had with a married man when she was only twenty. Alone on holidays and weekends, she was miserable in addition to being naïve---it is not a pleasant memory.

In her heart of hearts, she knows she will fare better in this relationship than she did with the other. She loves Deke and he loves her. Once his kids have adjusted to their relationship, she and Deke will have more time together---maybe someday they'll be a real family! A terrifying thought, she actually shudders!

She decides to workout before the Packer game at noon. Idly, she wonders if Deke is a Packer fan? Before she heads to the Y, she texts Deke—"go, pack, go" her message reads.

At the Y, she climbs on the elliptical and hits it hard for forty minutes. She is perspiring profusely when Deke and Andy walk in! She didn't even know they were members of the Y! They don't see her and she watches them walk through on their way to the pool. On their way out, an hour later, Andy spots her!

"Look daddy, it's…it's…" Andy can't seem to remember her name.

"Who, Andy?" Deke questions impatiently.

"You know, daddy—the whore." The moment that word slips out of his mouth, Andy tries to reclaim it from thin air!

Deke looks entirely disgusted with his offspring. He does not say a word. He merely takes Andy's hand, and walks straight out the door. Cress imagines there will be some serious conversation in the car on the way home between father and son.

"It's not really his fault," she defends. "His grandma introduced him to that word. Unfortunately, he's taken quite a shine to it."

She would smile if her feelings weren't so hurt.

After a cool shower, Cress wanders into The Wonder Bar, where she'll watch the first half of the game. She climbs up on a barstool and orders a beer. Green and gold is everywhere she looks! These are serious fans; they watch and react to the game, which is why she likes it. Free jello shots for touchdowns and loud cheering every time the Packers score.

An extremely hot male bartender makes a point of bringing Cress a shot every touchdown.

"New here?" he asks.

"Not really; I come in for Packer games."

"I usually close on Sunday nights. That must be how I've missed you. I would have remembered you." He gives her the once-over to reinforce his words.

"Right back at you," she flirts.

"What's your name?" he asks.

"Cress and you?"

"Stone." He acts a little embarrassed by his name and Cress can see why. She fights an urge to laugh.

"Uh-uh!"

"I know. It's queer, isn't it?"

"Your parents apparently didn't think so."

"They are the only two people in the universe who do not think it's queer and I think my mom might be wavering."

Cress chuckles. "I suppose that means you won't name your child Stone?"

"Damn right I won't saddle him with that stupid name!"

"Aww, it's not that bad."

"Seriously?"

"No." She giggles.

"Good, I didn't think you looked that dumb."

"Is that some kind of half-assed compliment because seriously, I'm not feeling the warmth?"

Stone went to the other end of the bar. For a minute she thought he was mad but he was just pouring a beer. Burdening a kid with a name like that was mean as hell, Cress thinks. In another lifetime, she may have tried to make it up to this good looking bartender with the queer name.

"That was then, this is now," she reminds herself, dedicating her attention to the Packers. From that point on, she gives him the cold shoulder.

"Married, huh?" He says after three unsuccessful tries at engaging her.

"Not married but definitely taken," she confesses.

"So you're saying I still have a chance?" He jokes.

"'Fraid not."

"Just my luck." He mumbles.

After the Packers wipe up the field with the Bears, Cress heads home. One more sleep and she will see her beloved! But what do with her evening? It really is like going with a married man; she thinks and she's not digging it!

CHAPTER 17

Getaway-Getaway!!

*M*onday and Cress is ready, waiting, and willing to see her love! Punctual, as always, Deke is right on time. Tenderly, he takes Cress in his arms.

"You cannot know how I've missed you---my weekend was so lonely, honey."

"I know a little bit about that, Deke---at least you have the kids."

"What did you do all weekend?" For the first time, he wonders how she fills her hours without him.

"Worked out, missed you, watched the game, missed you, turned in my story, missed you."

"We have to improve on this situation, Cress. I don't like leaving you alone every weekend and I miss you when I'm not here."

"Not much to be done right now," she says realistically.

"I'll think of something---this pace is killing me. The kids will have to toughen up a bit."

"Deke this should be done with finesse. Let them get used to the idea of me being in their lives."

"We've been doing that for over a month," he says impatiently.

"Gosh Deke, four years ago, they lost their mother---please don't shove me down their throats."

"I know you're right but I am tired of waiting to have my own life."

Cress pulls at his sports jacket. "Maybe I can make that life a little more tolerable," she suggests, backing him up till he is sitting on her bed.

"If you can't, no one can." He says, appreciatively.

As she loosens his tie, he puts his hands under her shirt, squeezing the bounty he finds there. "Do these always stand straight out like this?" he asks, gently gripping erect nipples.

"Only when you're here. That would be uncomfortable, always having rocklike nips rubbing against my shirts and bras."

"That's why athletes put band aids over theirs when they workout."

"If you're here much longer, I may have to try that."

"What if I just lick them when they get sore?" To demonstrate, he takes the rigid nodule in his mouth and sucks hungrily. His hands work down her skirt until she is before him in all her splendor and a top that is askew. She lifts the top over her head and dares him to touch her!

Deke takes that dare and tumbles her onto the bed. He positions himself between her legs and presses downward.

"Deke, your pants."

"They are a nuisance, aren't they?" he asks, shedding them.

Finally, they are once again skin-to-skin with a whole weekend to make up for. Cress is so anxious for him; she literally bucks upward in an effort to get him where she needs him. He is quick to pick up on her signals and swiftly enters her moistness.

"Each time, it's brand new," he exclaims. "You always feel so damn good."

"Deke," she says breathlessly. "Deke!"

Deacon speeds up until Cress is completely satisfied. He collapses on top of her, not enough energy to roll off. Just when he thinks he's recovered enough to roll away, her hips begin a slow, steady roll. When he thinks he can't, he finds he can---and he does!

His hand slides between them and his fingers skim over the sweet spot. She arches so violently, his hand becomes wedged between them. It intensifies each stroke and the pleasure goes on and on. No need to hurry this time; it will happen when it's meant to happen. When it does, it's spectacular!

"You're trying to make my kids orphans aren't you?" Deke grunts.

"Just the opposite," she promises.

"I have never had this much success in the sack, Cress." Deke admits shyly.

"What do you mean, honey?"

"In the past, even when I was a young stud, I was good for once, maybe twice a night. With you, I'm good for twice an hour and I'm an old man!"

"Old man, my ass!" Cress objects. "Could an old man make me feel the way you do? Could an old man make me shudder from the inside out?"

"Perhaps not old, but definitely seasoned. But if I am man enough for you, Cress I am the happiest guy on the planet!"

"You are such a fine man, such a great father, such a splendid and giving lover---I've never had better and I want no other, Deke. That's the truth!"

Deke kisses her deeply, intensely. Slowly, they rekindle. Cress feels something hard poking her in the hip and it appears, Deke is ready for round three! He is astonishing!

"Up here, Deke," she coaxes.

Not sure what is expected of him, Deke rises on all fours. Cress pulls him towards the headboard and he realizes what she means for him to do. Knees on either side of her head, Deke bends until Cress can take him in her mouth. Her arms are caught under him, she's essentially trapped, a thing that is oddly exciting. Deke has complete control over her as he moves down and back; slowly at first.

Cress's hands lie uselessly on her belly. While he gently, but thoroughly assaults her mouth, her hands slide down between her legs. She pleasures herself while Deke gently pummels her oral cavity. Her hips move in conjunction with his until she climaxes and he soon follows. It may go down as the best orgasm of her life and she tells Deke so!

"I think that every time," he chuckles. "You are a wonder."

"I wonder how I will get through till the next lunch hour," she says sadly.

"Don't give up honey---we'll figure this out."

"So you say."

Deke gets up and redresses; he feels like a million bucks; so relaxed, so happy, so lucky! "Just call me, Mr. Lucky!"

"You'll be lucky to have a job if you don't get back to work," she advises.

"I'll call you tonight," he says, disappearing out the front door.

Cress wonders if she is insatiable; she simply can't get enough of Deke's lovemaking!

"Dad," Shelby asks at the dinner table. "Where has Cress been? You didn't break up, did you?"

"No, nothing like that—was that the answer you hoped for?"

"Dad, just wondering." Shelby did the unthinkable; she rolled her eyes at her dad! It was a first and Deke didn't think much of it.

"Was that really necessary, Shel?"

"I'm sorry, dad but you act like I have something against Cress and I don't."

"Good to know, Shel because this weekend, Cress and I will be going away. Netta will stay with you and Andy and of course, Kiya may stay, as well."

"You mean overnight, dad?" She is scandalized.

"A Bed and Breakfast, I think is what they call them." He seems calm but inside he is worried stiff!

"Well, that's just embarrassing!" With flushed cheeks, Shelby stomps out of the room.

Cress's reaction to this news is similar to his daughters. She is embarrassed for the teenager to learn of their pending intimacy. "I thought we agreed we would go slow."

"Honey, we've been going so slow, we're going backwards!"

Despite the objections of the women, Deke personally books their room— for two nights! He kisses confused children and feeling like a heel, leaves to collect Cress.

"Daddy, are you coming back to read my story?"

"Maybe Shelby will do it---just this once, son."

"No story?" Andy looks stricken.

"We'll read two on Sunday—I promise Andy."

Deke has never missed a bedtime story before. He wonders what Marissa would think of this? He is subdued on the drive up north; Cress allows him to stew in his own guilt. He wears his guilt like a hair shirt.

Deke leads her to a quaint little suite as though he is going before a firing squad. In their room, he tries to lighten things up by bouncing on the bed. Cress follows his lead but it sure doesn't feel like a holiday.

"Are you hungry, honey?"

"I could eat."

"Whoa; you're enthusiasm is underwhelming."

"Pot. Kettle. Black."

"Pardon?"

"You are the pot calling the kettle black."

"I know. I just can't shake the feeling that I am abandoning the kids as surely as Marissa did."

"Deke, what prompted this romantic getaway? I don't recall pressuring you."

"I felt we were stagnating; I wanted to light a fire under our relationship."

"How's that working for you?"

"Not very damn well."

"Go home, Deke."

"No honey, I want to have some alone-time with you."

"At whose expense? You can't think I want you with me if it makes Shelby and Andy miserable? Please, go home."

"Are you sure?"

"One hundred percent sure. This is not how we find happiness, Deke—not by making the children unhappy."

"You are one in a million, Cress. Thank you for understanding."

"Don't act so surprised, Deke. I'm not some kind of monster."

"So---you're pissed?"

"Absolutely but not for the reasons you think."

"What, then?"

"You orchestrate this whole thing without asking me. You get us all shook up and for what? I didn't need a Bed and Breakfast, Deke. You were feeling guilty about me and now you're feeling guilty about the kids—where does it get any of us?"

"I wanted to wow and surprise you, Cress."

"You wow me every time we're together. Just drop me off and go home to the kids, Deke."

"Are you sure?"

"Please go home and reassure your kids." She instructs before she disappears inside.

Deke has to admit he is driving home with a lighter heart. He is anxious to see the kids although he has been gone only a matter of hours. It's almost as if Andy is waiting by the window for him to arrive. Before he turns off the car, Andy is running towards him.

"I knew you'd come back, daddy!"

"I was always coming back, Andy. I will always come back to you, son."

"I know, daddy," Andy says, rubbing his head against his father's arm.

Shelby met them in the foyer. "Andy, I told you not to go outside without telling me!" she scolds.

"He was just meeting me, Shel."

"Dad if you expect me to take care of him, you need to back me up!"

"I know but is it possible you're overreacting, just a tad?"

"Do you know how scared I was when I went in his room?" Her bottom lip quivers and Deke can see she is really bothered---by something.

"I'll have a talk with him tonight, honey."

Deke offers Netta the rest of the weekend off. She jumps at the opportunity, stopping only long enough to kiss the children goodbye. Over cold cut sandwiches, Shelby finally summons the courage to ask her dad what happened.

"Missed you guys," he admits.

"Yeah, sure."

"I guess I'm just not ready, Shel."

"Wait—what? You're not ready? How does Cress feel about this?"

"She insisted I come home."

"She did?"

"Even grown-ups get homesick, honey. Cress saw that I was homesick so she sent me home!"

"I suppose she was mad."

"Maybe at me."

"Why, dad? You just wanted to take her away for the weekend."

"Whose side are you on, anyhow?"

"What do you mean?"

"First, you're mad I go away, then you're mad when I come home, and now you're mad because Cress sent me home to you."

"Dad, I know but it was so unexpected---you never left us before."

"Shelby I'm as confused as you are."

"What about Cress, dad? Do you love her?"

"I do," he sighs.

"Then, why so sad?"

"Some days it seems hopeless."

"Because of me and Andy?"

"No honey, because of the grown-ups involved. I'm ready to move it up a notch but she's balking."

"What do you mean, move it up a notch? Do you want to marry Cress?"

"I don't know, cookie. I'm ready to go there but are you and Andy ready? Is Cress?"

"I don't know how to answer that, dad. Let me think about it; we've been alone around here so long, it would be weird to have someone else around."

"It would be an adjustment, that's for sure."

"We wouldn't have to call her mom, would we, dad?"

"Uh, no. Only one mom to a customer, Shel."

"One is all I ever wanted, daddy," she sniffles, hugging Deke. "Remember when you felt that way?"

"Shelby, you think I've forgotten your mother? If it were up to me, we would go back five years when it was you, mom, Andy, and me. I would have been content with that arrangement for the rest of my life but that just isn't going to happen!"

"Dad, do you love Cress more than you loved mom?" Shelby was asking the hard questions, the ones that have plagued her since Deke first mentioned Cress.

"It isn't like I ever stopped loving your mom, honey. I still do; she was wonderful and the perfect mate for me until that mean, bastardly disease took her away. I miss your mother everyday but miracles of miracles, I was sent someone else to love, to share my life!"

"And?"

"What is a living, breathing man to do, Shelby? Cling tenaciously to a corpse or meet the second love of his life head-on? My loving Cress does not mean I don't love you guys or your mom, Shel."

"Okay dad," Shelby simply says, exiting the room.

"Shel---are we done here?"

"I have some thinking to do, dad!"

"As do we all," Deke muses.

CHAPTER 18

Selfless Love

*M*onday morning, Cress will get a new number, she has decided. If necessary, she will move to avoid *contact with Deke* when all she really wants is *contact with Deke!*

"I won't do this to him anymore," she resolves. "The poor guy is walking a tightrope, trying to appease the kids and me and maybe even his mother-in-law. I can't do it to him anymore," she sobs.

She mopes all weekend and ignores his calls. Finally she turns her phone off entirely and feels like she is playing some queer high school bargaining game--except she's not. Like a rare captured bird, Cress is setting Deke free and someday he will appreciate it, she hopes.

"Don't hate me, Deke," she whispers in the empty apartment. "I'd hold on fiercely but I love you too much to put you through this anymore."

Deke is entirely frazzled to the point he actually wonders if all this chaos is really worth it. He imagines the beautiful Cress; those intelligent eyes looking at him, her utter acceptance of everyone, her quirky humor, and her extraordinary capacity for love. For the sixth time today, he tries her number. He just wants to hear her voice and reassure her he will make this work somehow.

"Dammit!" he says hearing it go to Voicemail once again.

"What's wrong daddy?"

"Oh Andy, your old man is a blooming idiot!" He says, absent mindedly.

"My daddy is not idiot!" Andy says indignantly. "My daddy is smarter than Bama!"

"Smarter than who, Andy?" Deke grins.

"He's talking about the President, dad," Shelby says. "And he's right."

"Thanks for the vote of confidence, kids," Deke says with a heavy heart.

"What's wrong, dad?"

"I'm okay, don't worry about me."

"Is it Cress?"

"Honey, I got this. You just worry about Miss Kiya."

"Dad," Shelby goes to her father. "Do you think Andy and I can be happy if you're not?"

"Of course not. I know we're all in this together." Deke hugs Shelby and Andy wedges his way in between them.

"Hey, let's get out of the house! Does anyone want ice cream?"

Andy's bouncing tells Deke he has made an excellent suggestion. Shelby goes along, just being a good sport.

"Want to call Kiya?" Deke asks.

"I'm good with you boys, dad."

The line at the DQ extends to the curb. "Do you want to go into the city?" Deke asks.

The kids agree and Deke drives to Mad-city. He goes to the ice cream parlor where he and Cress got cones on their big date. Ordering, her glares at the young man Cress knows---how well does he know her, Deke wonders.

They sit on a bench out front and eat their ice cream. "You guys want to walk around State Street? Look in the store windows?"

His kids decline, surprising Deke. "Where does Cress live, dad? Near here?"

"Why?" Deke asks suspiciously.

"Just curious."

"She's over on West Wilson."

"Want to stop in, dad?"

"Since she's not answering my calls, I don't think any kind of drop-in would be appropriate, honey."

Shelby is inwardly outraged that Cress will not speak to her father! Who does she think she is, anyhow? More importantly, who does Deke think she is? Someone pretty important to him, it seems. She cannot bear to see her only parent so unhappy but she is powerless to do anything about it.

Some sort of thumping is what Deke hears at 8 a.m. Sunday morning. Thump—thump---thump, it's coming from somewhere close---his closet!

"What the hell?" he wonders.

Shelby seems to be in his closet; that's more than a little weird. "Shel, what are you doing in there? Today is the day we all sleep in!"

"Oh sorry, dad. You've been after me for two years to clean this closet and go through mom's stuff."

"And you've chosen today to do it?" He is groggy from lack of sleep.

"Seemed like a good time, dad."

"For whom?" Deke asks, sitting on the side of the bed. Looking down, he notices he is only in boxers. It's rare the kids come in his room and he doesn't want to gross Shelby out by walking past her in his skivvies.

"Shel, avert your face, I am in my boxers."

Shelby laughs at her father's modesty and continues going through her mother's clothing, shoes, and purses. There is much to go through and nothing Shelby wants for herself. Too retro for the trendy Shelby!

"Most of this can be donated, dad. We have a closet at my school. Kids that are homeless or in need of anything, get to take what they want for free. I think mom would like us to donate it to kids who need it."

"Indeed she would. But honey, tell me again, why are we doing this today?"

"Well dad," she says shyly. "I thought Cress would need the extra room."

"Cress? What does Cress need with room in my closet?"

"Dad," Shelby says in her no-nonsense voice. "Cress will need her own space when she moves in!"

Deke is wide awake now. "Did you say when she moves in, Shel?"

"Dad, that's what you want, isn't it?"

"Uhmmmm…"

"Is that what Cress wants, dad?"

"I don't know, truthfully."

"Maybe take a ride and find out, dad because Andy and I are cool with it."

"You and Andy are cool with Cress moving in?" Deke is in a complete daze.

"And don't worry about grandma, dad. I've already had a talk with her. If she continues to give Cress a hard time, she won't be able to see me and Andy."

"You've been a busy girl, Miss Shelby. Thank you!

Now it's entirely up to Cress to decide…"

www.ingramcontent.com/pod-product-compliance
Lightning Source LLC
Chambersburg PA
CBHW051709170526
45167CB00002B/597